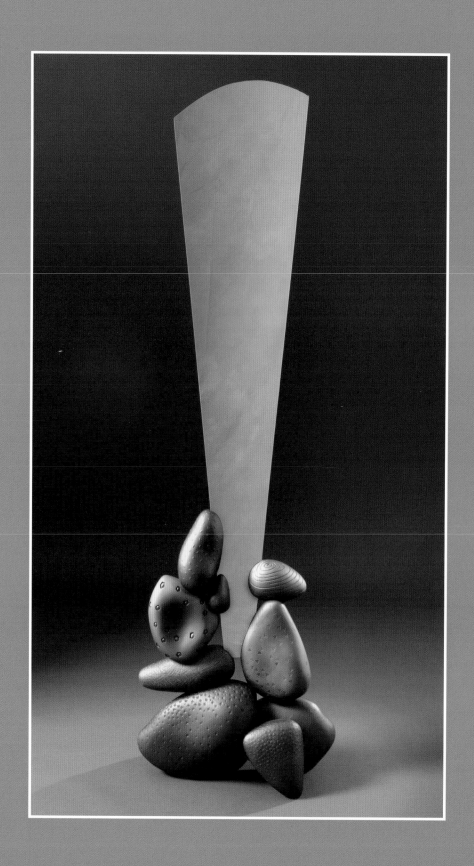

The Penland Book
of Woodworking

Master Classes in
Woodworking Techniques

LARK BOOKS

A Division of
Sterling Publishing Co., Inc.
New York

Library of Congress Cataloging-in-Publication Data

The Penland book of woodworking : master classes in woodworking techniques /
Thomas W. Stender, editor.— 1st ed.
p. cm.
Includes index.
ISBN 1-57990-768-7 (hardcover)
1. Woodwork. I. Stender, Thomas W., 1947- II. Penland School of Crafts.
III. Title.
TT180.P42 2007
684'.08—dc22
2006006317

10 9 8 7 6 5 4 3 2 1

First Edition

Published by Lark Books, A Division of
Sterling Publishing Co., Inc.
387 Park Avenue South, New York, N.Y. 10016

Text and illustrations © 2006 Lark Books
Photography © 2006 Lark Books, or as noted

Distributed in Canada by Sterling Publishing,
c/o Canadian Manda Group, 165 Dufferin Street
Toronto, Ontario, Canada M6K 3H6

Distributed in the United Kingdom by GMC Distribution Services,
Castle Place, 166 High Street, Lewes, East Sussex, England BN7 1XU

Distributed in Australia by Capricorn Link (Australia) Pty Ltd.,
P.O. Box 704, Windsor, NSW 2756 Australia

If you have questions or comments about this book, please contact:
Lark Books
67 Broadway
Asheville, NC 28801
(828) 253-0467

Manufactured in China

ISBN 13: 978-1-57990-768-6
ISBN 10: 1-57990-768-7

For information about custom editions, special sales, premium and corpo-
rate purchases, please contact Sterling Special Sales Department at 800-
805-5489 or specialsales@sterlingpub.com.

Editor: Thomas Stender
Art Director: Kristi Pfeffer
Cover Designer: Barbara Zaretsky
Associate Editor: Nathalie Mornu
Associate Art Director: Shannon Yokeley
Art Production Assistant: Jeff Hamilton
Editorial Assistance: Dawn Dillingham,
    Delores Gosnell, Rosemary Kast
Editorial Interns: Megan Taylor Cox,
    David Squires, Sue Stigleman

Photo credits
Cover: Jere Osgood, *Bubinga Shell Desk,* 1985
Page 1: Paul M. Sasso, *Lil' Yellow Table,* 2005
Page 2: Brent Skidmore, *Maxwell's Mellow
Mirror,* 2005
Page 5: Craig Nutt, *Radish Salad Bowl,* 1998
Pages 8, 9, 212, and 213: all photos
© Penland School of Crafts

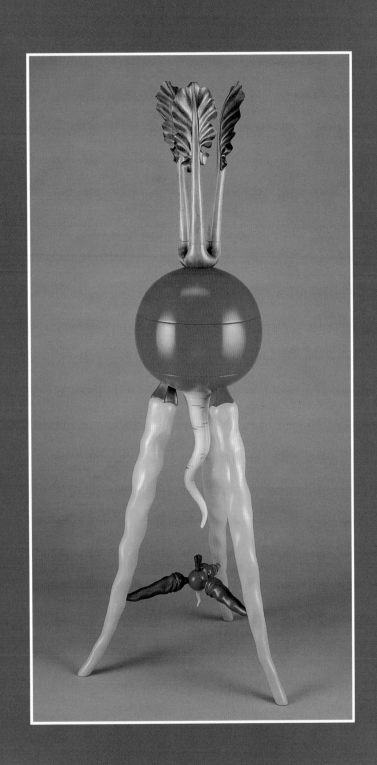

Contents

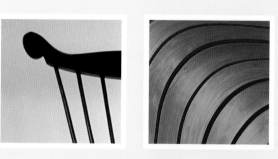

Introduction

The *Penland Book of Woodworking* is the fourth volume in a series produced by Lark Books in collaboration with Penland School of Crafts. The two institutions are neighbors in the Southern Appalachian region of North Carolina, and this series brings together some of their most important resources: Lark's many years of producing books to guide and inspire artists of all levels and Penland's national community of artist teachers.

This book has several functions: to give the reader insight into the creative and technical processes of leading woodworkers, to provide detailed, intermediate-level technical information, and to showcase a range of approaches to the material. To that end, each of the contributing artists was asked to write an essay which might talk about their personal history, their education, their sources of inspiration and motivation, or aspects of the technique which is the focus of their chapter. These essays are liberally illustrated with examples of each artist's work. They are followed by a hands-on section which provides step-by-step instructions in a particular technique. Each chapter concludes with a gallery section highlighting the work of other artists who practice the same technique or whose work has been meaningful for the author of that chapter. What we hope to create

is a technical and inspirational resource for anyone interested in contemporary woodworking practice.

The first woodworking class at Penland, taught in 1942, promised to give students at least enough skill to keep a loom adjusted and repaired—a close tie-in with the school's origins as a weaving institute. Several years later, Penland began to include carving and whittling as part of its array of folk crafts. Woodcarving (an old photograph shows reliefs and figurines) and making wooden shepherd's pipes were listed in the Penland catalogs until 1962, the year the school's founder Lucy Morgan retired. She was succeeded by Bill Brown, who reshaped Penland's program in the 1960s. In his first year at Penland, Brown invited woodworker C.R. "Skip" Johnson to come and teach classes in furniture building. He was soon joined by Doug Sigler—one of the contributors to this book—and the two of them taught every summer into the 1980s. During this time, Penland began to attract some of the most important craft artists in the country and the Penland wood program was shaped by the same kind of inspired makers who are represented in this book.

Today, the program emphasizes sculpture as well as furniture, encompassing areas such as design, joinery, surface treatment, laminated and bent

wood, upholstery, greenwood techniques, cabinetry, figurative sculpture, carving, and mixed-media. Recent offerings have included classes in site-specific work, guitar building, boatbuilding and carving with tools ranging from chisels to die grinders to chainsaws. Although the artists featured in this book are mostly furniture makers, a number of them create work which blurs the distinction between furniture and sculpture, and readers will find many techniques here which are applicable to both areas.

The topics for this book were selected to create a balance between structural and decorative techniques. Michael Puryear, Doug Sigler, and Jere Osgood explore different methods of lamination to create curved forms, and Curtis Buchanan demonstrates his method for assembling a traditional Windsor chair. Paul Sasso and Jenna Goldberg explore very different approaches to applying color, Brent Skidmore explains some of his surface texturing methods, John Clark breaks down his technique for inlaid veneer, and Kurt Nielsen explores his process for creating carved figures. Craig Nutt takes a step back from the bench to talk about how he develops designs using models and digital technology.

One of the great strengths of a workshop-based program is that it gives students access to instruction by full-time studio artists who do not teach classes on a regular basis and by university faculty who are generally available only to students enrolled in their university programs. Penland teaches classes in books and paper, clay, drawing and painting, glass, iron, metals, printmaking, photography, textiles, and wood, and all of our students benefit from having these media taught side by side. Not only is it useful to see ideas being shaped by different materials, it's no surprise to find a bookbinder in the woodshop getting help with a wooden book cover or to see a piece of furniture embellished with hammered copper from one of the metals classes. Inspiration at Penland also comes from having students of different ages, backgrounds, and levels of experience working together to explore an interest they hold in common. The special learning environment at Penland has, over many years, created a community among the people who teach and learn at the school. It is our hope that these books will bring some of the knowledge and passion contained in that community to a wider circle.

We are grateful to the artist-authors for their knowledge, their thoughtful writing, and their beautiful work. They have already contributed to the field through making and teaching, and this book will extend those contributions. Thanks also to Dana Moore, Penland's point person on this project, and Robin Dreyer, Penland's communications director, to Thomas Stender, Kristi Pfeffer, Carol Taylor, and everyone else at Lark Books who put it all together. Special thanks go to Rob Pulleyn, Lark's founder and past president, for bringing this series of books to life.

I feel sure that *The Penland Book of Woodworking* will bring new ideas and inspiration to your work with this marvelous material.

Jean W. McLaughlin
Director, Penland School of Crafts

Craig Nutt

Combining sketching, model making, digital imaging, and hand coloring, Craig Nutt's design process provides both relative precision and wide flexibility. By carving scale models, including hinged doors and decorative elements, he can revise a form in three dimensions. Digital photographs of the model, printed in grayscale, enable him to try various color combinations and formal details. This level of preparation allows Craig to make his witty vegetable furniture with speed and assurance. The finished work always looks as if it somehow had grown that way, thereby pulling the viewer willy-nilly into a semi-surreal world where such things are all too normal.

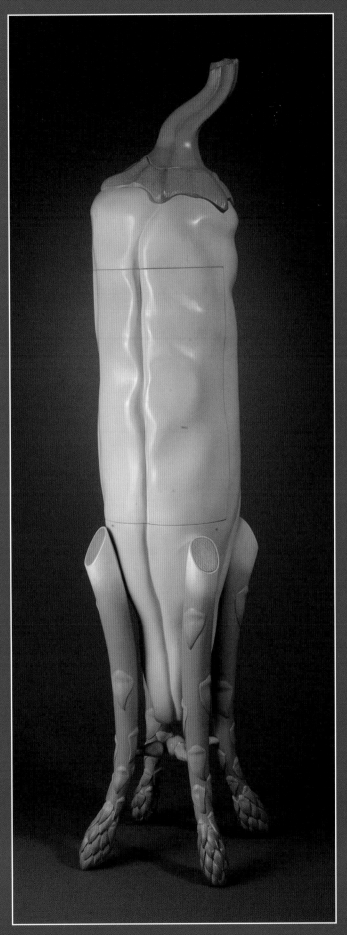

CRAIG NUTT
*Banana Pepper Cabinet with
Seeds and Fruit*, 2001

81 x 17 x 17 inches
(205.7 x 43.2 x 43.2 cm)
Wood, oil paint, lacquer; carved
PHOTO © JOHN LUCAS

Vegetable Bebop and Tut Uncommon

The transition from making traditional furniture to the more personal and sculptural furniture that I make now was one of the most challenging and important in my career. I have heard it said that sailing is hours of total bliss punctuated by moments of sheer terror. It seems that my work has followed a similar rhythm of deliberate evolution punctuated by periodic insights. That mixture of evolution and revelation characterize my struggle to integrate my art with my craft.

From about 1970 until the early '80s I was fortunate to be involved with a collective of artists in Tuscaloosa, Alabama, known as Raudelunas, and like some of the others in the group, I was an aspiring painter. If Raudelunas had a uniting principle it was openness to experimentation—no idea was considered too strange, absurd, or outrageous to try. Whatever the vision for an artwork, performance, or piece of music, one was likely to find some help in realizing it and a small but receptive audience—a considerable encouragement for someone working in the conservative Deep South at the time.

More often than not, Raudelunas projects took the form of improvised music. This was music free of any preconceived structure, musical clichés, riffs, tonality, and other constraints of traditional music. Many of us had been inspired by the free jazz of musicians such as John Coltrane and Ornette Coleman, but also were influenced by composers such as John Cage, Karlheinz Stockhausen, and Harry Partch, and by blues musicians such as Johnny Shines and Fred McDowell. We were attempting to create a music that was totally spontaneous and open to all kinds of sound. At the time, lacking a more precise description, I thought of it as a sculptural approach to music. As we

CRAIG NUTT
Burning, 2002
46 x 57 x 31 inches (116.8 x 144.8 x 78.7 cm)
Tulip poplar, oil paint, acrylic lacquer, chenille fabric hand woven by Janet Taylor with dye vat discharge; carved, joined
PHOTOS © JOHN LUCAS

explored this musical experiment and produced some records, we gradually discovered similar enclaves of people who had been doing the same thing in Europe and around the States.

Most of us admired the Dadaists, Surrealists, and the early 20th-century French playwright Alfred Jarry and his "science" of pataphysics, the science of imaginary solutions. "Imaginary solutions" is a key phrase because that was a period of unbridled imagination. I would characterize the later work of all of the artists involved with the Raudelunas group as highly imaginative, and the experience was a major influence on the direction of my own work.

I graduated from the University of Alabama in 1972 and found a job working in an antique shop that had refinishing, restoration, and upholstery departments. When I took that job, I knew virtually

CRAIG NUTT
Nine Carrot Treasure Chest, 2002

94 x 20 x 20 inches (238.8 x 50.8 x 50.8 cm)
Walnut, maple, tulip poplar, oil paint, acrylic lacquer, brass,
glass, lighting; turned, carved, dovetailed
PHOTOS © JOHN LUCAS

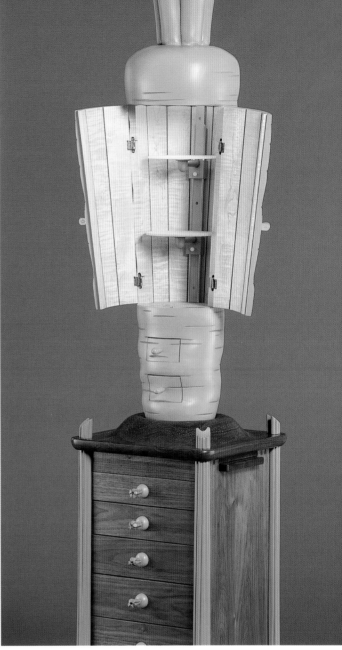

nothing about furniture, whether historical or contemporary. I simply never had given furniture much thought. But in taking pieces of furniture apart to repair them and in making missing pieces, I became intrigued with the construction techniques and with furniture styles. Initially, it was something of a detective process, learning by inference. "These are the tools they had, here are the marks of the tools on the wood, and there must be only two or three ways that they could have made these dovetails." Some of the pieces I worked on were well over 100 years old, still strong and easily repaired, while much newer, mass-produced pieces were already broken and not worth fixing.

This experience reacquainted me with the ethic of craftsmanship. In retrospect, this was something I think my parents and grandparents had tried to teach me. But I grew up in the postwar consumer culture of cheap manufactured goods and planned obsolescence. We were making disposable goods for a disposable planet. Craftsmanship seemed like an antidote to that kind of thinking, and I think that is why those old pieces of furniture resonated with me. It seems terribly naive to see it in print, but I thought that maybe the first step in making a nondisposable planet was to make things as if they would be passed down to future generations. At least it might turn out to be a personally rewarding and interesting career.

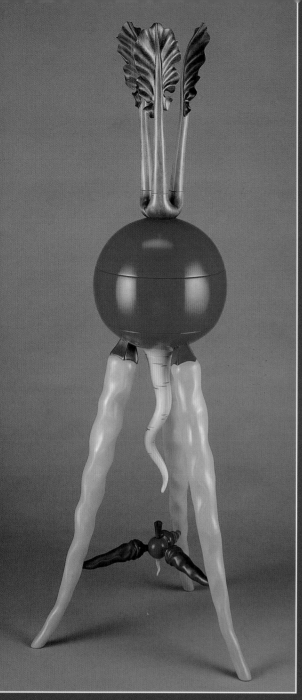

CRAIG NUTT
Radish Salad Bowl, 1998

56 x 21 x 17 inches (142.2 x 53.3 x 43.2 cm)
Bleached maple, lacquer; turned, carved
PHOTOS © JOHN LUCAS
COLLECTION OF THE RENWICK GALLERY OF THE SMITHSONIAN AMERICAN ART
MUSEUM, WASHINGTON, DC

CRAIG NUTT
Radish Table, 2004

29 x 24 x 24 inches (73.7 x 61 x 61 cm)
Bleached maple, tulip poplar, oil paint; turned, bent
laminated, carved
PHOTOS © JOHN LUCAS

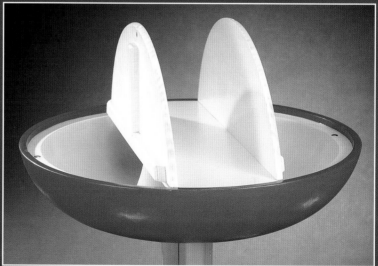

By day I was a mild-mannered period furniture maker, totally absorbed by my craft, and in my spare time I was painting, playing improvised music, and acting as an impresario of the avant garde. It was a bit schizoid, but initially it was easy to separate my art from my craft, and I was pretty sure that my furniture clients would not appreciate the music and paintings I was making. As time passed I became more absorbed in furniture making and woodworking. Increasingly, I depended on the challenges of learning my craft and working within a period furniture genre for my creative outlet while doing less painting and experimental work. I had a local market in Alabama that was solidly oriented to period styles, and there was an endless supply of antiques that needed help. However, by the late '70s I was starting to feel that period furniture might be a creative dead end for me, and I felt that I needed to move beyond technique with my work. While most of my work consisted of adaptations of period styles and were not direct copies, I started working on more original designs while still making period style pieces on commission.

In 1978 and 1979 two events had a major effect on the direction of my furniture designs. The first was the blockbuster exhibition, "The Treasures of Tutankhamen." The furniture in that exhibition, especially the small ebony throne, completely changed my view of furniture. These pieces were more than 3,000 years old, but the joints were the same mortise-and-tenon and dovetail joints with which I was familiar. I had been looking mostly at western furniture from the 18th and 19th centuries. Animal and plant motifs were common but were used in a decorative way to embellish legs and aprons. A typical table might have four cabriole legs with ball-and-claw feet, each identical and each facing out from its respective corner. The Egyptian furniture was much more naturalistic. With its elegant front paws and haunch-like rear legs,

Tut's feline throne looked as if it could walk across the room. I was accustomed to the construction of legs joined by aprons, but many of the chairs, tables, and beds in this exhibition had legs mortised into the bottoms of frames. This was a strong and stable construction that eliminated visually heavy aprons that might have interfered with the lines of the legs. As I stood there in the New Orleans Museum of Art, transfixed by that little chair, I did not realize how important that construction detail would become to my work, but I did know that my perception of furniture had changed.

In 1979 the first of two wood conferences took place at the newly opened Purchase College, north of New York City. The traditional furniture presentations on the program convinced me to buy a plane ticket, but once I got there it was the more adventurous work that captured my imagination.

CRAIG NUTT
Tomato Table, 1996

26 x 23 x 23 inches (66 x 58.4 x 58.4 cm)
Tulip poplar, dyed veneer, blood wood, maple, oil paint; turned, carved, marquetry
PHOTO © RICKEY YANAURA
COLLECTION OF THE COLUMBUS MUSEUM, COLUMBUS, GA

CRAIG NUTT
Corncorde, 1996

36 x 120 x 120 inches (91.4 x 304.8 x 304.8 cm)
Tulip poplar, oil paint; laminated, turned, carved
PHOTO © ARTIST
COMMISSIONED FOR THE HARTSFIELD-JACKSON ATLANTA INTERNATIONAL
AIRPORT, ATLANTA, GA

This was the first time I had spent time with other furniture makers of my generation, and it was such a rewarding experience that I went back the next year. (It was 17 years before another gathering of this scope—the first Furniture Society conference— took place. Again it was at SUNY Purchase, and I helped organize it.)

Seeing the slide presentations in 1979 and 1980, hearing makers talk about their work, and talking with other makers between sessions opened my eyes to the creative potential of furniture. I started to think that furniture could be art just as surely as was painting or sculpture. Why couldn't a work of art incorporate craftsmanship, utility, and a craftsman's appreciation of materials? Why couldn't furniture be art? An art professor once told me, "Picasso

did the art world a great disservice by making pots—confusing art and craft." I admit that the idea of going against the grain of an art establishment that separated art and craft appealed to my more subversive impulses.

As I started to look at furniture as an art medium, essentially interchangeable with sculpture, I realized that furniture had considerable advantages over sculpture, notably the element of function and a wide variety of almost universally understood historical forms and styles. These elements offered rich subject matter that could be utilized. I would later realize just how rich a source furniture history is when my series of garden-themed wind sculptures, called "flying vegetables," became the beginning of furniture based on imagery from my vegetable garden. Historical furniture forms have written the subtext to many of the pieces I have made. While the historical references are respectful, they also satirize the prevalant, backward-looking tastes that mandate the manufacture of reproductions now, long after their time has gone.

Partly a legacy from the naturalistic pose of Tutankhamen's feline chair, vegetation became the structure of my furniture rather than an embellishment. Once a subscriber to the inviolability of the natural beauty of wood, I got beyond the old taboo against painting wood when in the mid '80s I did a series of turned vessels with colorful lacquered surfaces. Now I turned to oil paints and lacquers to represent the vegetables with clarity. Truth to the subject trumped truth to materials. I keep returning to the vegetable motif because it has developed into a personal and metaphorically rich vocabulary. These commonplace objects, at once products of nature and of human manipulation, taken out of their normal context and scale, invite a fresh look at other wonders that routine renders mundane. They lend themselves to absurdity, humor, beauty, and even dignity.

Initially my craft was primarily a way to make a living. The richness of furniture and the eloquence of craft revealed themselves gradually. When I stopped thinking of my art and my craft as separate pursuits, I was able to reach a synthesis that combined the creativity and spontaneity that I prized in art and music with the technique and values of craft. Looking back, it seems that this was my obvious destination, but it is also apparent that the route I took to get there profoundly affected both my work and myself.

CRAIG NUTT
Celery Chairs with Carrots, Peppers, and Snow Pea, 2005
37 x 19 x 22 inches (94 x 48.3 x 55.9 cm)
Tulip poplar, leather, acrylic lacquer; turned, carved
PHOTOS © DEBORAH WIYGUL

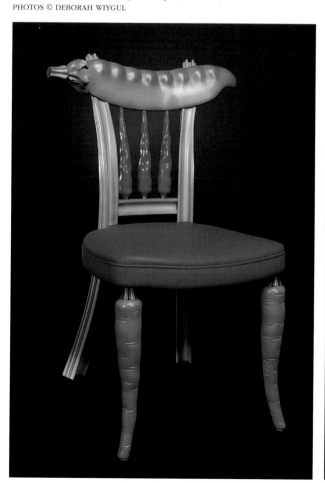

Hands On

Craig Nutt thinks of his maquettes as three-dimensional sketches. He uses them to test ideas, introduce spontaneity, and create client presentations, but he rarely submits a model as a final presentation. He prefers to photograph the maquette and then alter the photograph, trying out various details and doing color studies. Because the maquette itself will not be part of a presentation, he can make it quickly and focus on its value as a design tool, rather than as a finished object. Here he demonstrates the process from sketch to presentation drawings.

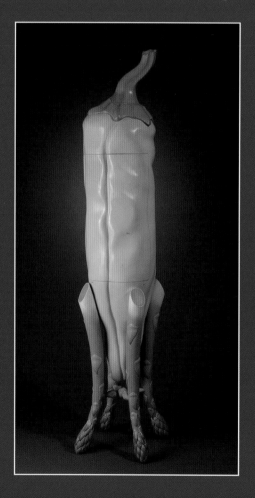

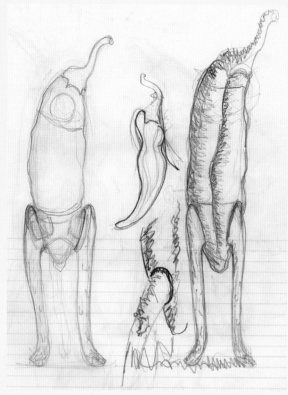

1. I record ideas for pieces in my sketchbook. The sketches typically are a mix of visual, functional, and construction details. Once I have worked out the major problems, I do a rough drawing to scale. Keep in mind that one advantage of making models is that working in three dimensions makes it easier to visualize the work and find solutions that would not have been seen while working on a flat page.

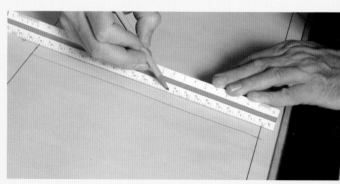

2. The scale drawing begins with layout lines indicating the overall size and transition points, such as the positions of legs and doors, etc. I often work on several versions of all or part of the piece simultaneously in order to try out different ideas. A drawing board with a parallel rule is helpful, but a T-square, a few triangles, and a compass are about all you really need.

A typical architect's scale is laid out in feet and inches, but it is more useful to assign each interval a value of 1 inch. The markings at each end of a face of the scale that normally indicate inches are used to roughly estimate fractions of an inch. So the ¼ scale, rather than indicating ¼ inch = 1 foot, now indicates ¼ size (sometimes indicated as 1:4 or one to four).

For large pieces, ⅛ size works well, and ¼ size is good for smaller pieces. I look for a size that will be small enough to construct quickly but large enough that smaller parts do not become too tiny to handle easily.

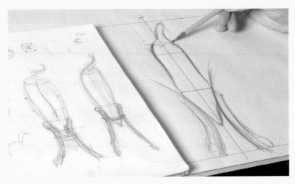

3. Once the layout lines are in place, I draw the piece to scale, using my sketchbook drawings as a rough guide. At this point, I pay close attention to how the parts will fit, how doors will open, etc.

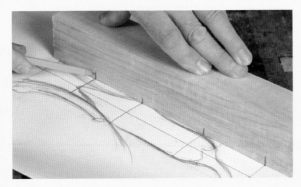

4. Marks for key parts of the cabinet model are transferred directly from the drawing to the wood. If I have to measure anything, I use the architect's scale, so I do not have to calculate. Poplar is used here because it is light in color and easy to work with. Basswood would also be a good choice (more about the color later).

5. A recess for the doors is cut with the bandsaw.

6. Then a block of wood for each door is hotglued back into the block. It should stick well enough to stay in while you're turning and carving but not so well that you can't get it out!

7. Anything that is nearly round is shaped on the lathe. Both the scale drawing and sketches serve as guides. At this point it is easy to change things—the drawings do not have the force of law.

8. Measurements can be taken directly from the scale drawing with calipers and transferred to the turning by using a parting tool.

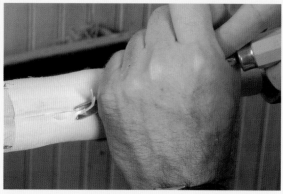

9. The lathe makes an excellent vise. As much carving as possible is done while the work is mounted on the lathe.

10. The doors are gently removed with a chisel.

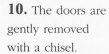

11. The inside of the cabinet is hollowed with a gouge.

12. The insides of the doors are hollowed in a similar way.

13. Now that the pepper no longer needs to be mounted on the lathe, the stem can be roughed out with a coping saw.

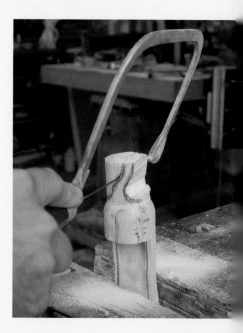

14. The stem and calyx are shaped with a gouge.

15. A Kevlar glove can help prevent cuts when you're carving with a knife or a small carving gouge. Files, rasps, and rifflers are also useful for shaping.

16. Sandpaper is also good for finer shaping and smoothing. I generally do not go much finer than 80 grit. I don't worry too much about tool marks either. These will not show in the photographs.

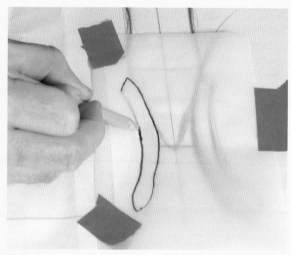

17. Drafting vellum or tracing paper is used to make a leg pattern from the scale drawing. I don't worry too much about fine details. These can be added to the photograph. Remember, this is a design tool, not the finished piece. Think of it as a three-dimensional sketch.

18. The traced leg is glued to some cardboard with spray adhesive, and a leg pattern is cut out. Some scale stock is cut for the legs. Again, I use an architect's scale, rather than calculating dimensions. This is much faster and less prone to error.

19. The legs are traced onto the scale lumber, sawed out, and shaped.

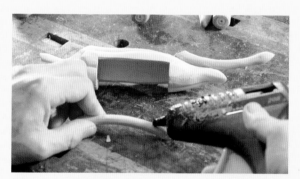

20. The legs are glued on with hot-melt adhesive.

21. The position of the legs is checked. If the position is wrong, or if I do not like the leg or another component, I just rip it off! It is easy to change the model or try other ideas now. It is hard when you get to the full-sized piece. This is the time to play—to improvise! I don't get too invested in the model; it's only jazz!

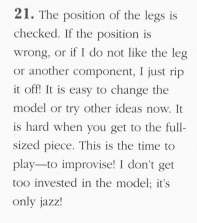

22. Stretcher parts were turned on the lathe. I might have left this detail out to draw in later, but it also helps to keep the model from falling apart.

23. The parts do not have to fit perfectly. The hot-melt glue will fill in the gaps, and the details will be fixed on the photograph. The model can be a bit rough, but I try not to be sloppy.

24. Small parts are glued in place and adjusted for clearance.

25. Hinges for the door are quick and dirty; they're made from bits of Tyvek.

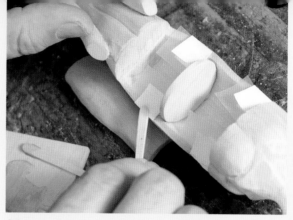

26. The hinges are glued to the cabinet with five-minute epoxy.

27. Then the hinges are glued to the doors.

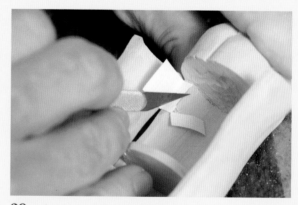

28. After the glue has dried, the excess paper is trimmed with a penknife.

29. What do you put inside a pepper cabinet? How would a cherry look?

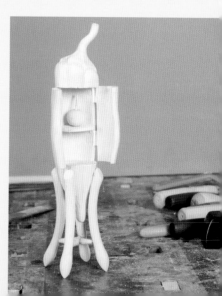

Craig Nutt

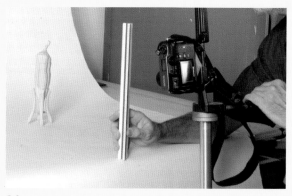

30. The piece is photographed against a feature-less background, in this case butcher paper. A scale room can also be mocked up from foam-board if needed. The scale is used to position the camera height so that the perspective is similar to how a full-sized piece would be photographed. I am using 60 scale inches to approximate how it would be viewed from a standing position.

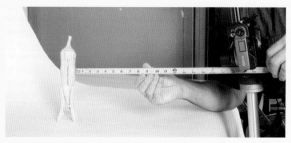

31. Distance from the camera is not as important as the height of the lens, but I try to keep it in the range of a normal viewing distance. Because the scale is not long enough for this measurement, I had to calculate the distance in inches.

32. I used to photograph with film, processing and printing before proceeding. Digital photography has really streamlined this process. The piece is photographed from different angles, in order to find positions that give as much information about the piece as possible.

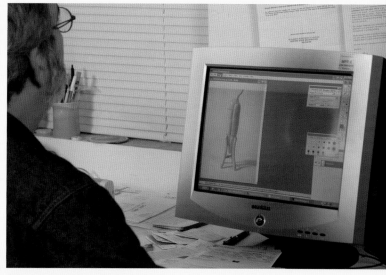

33. The image is loaded into an image manipulation program such as Photoshop or Paintshop. The image adjustment tools are used to convert the image to black and white and to adjust the lightness and contrast, resulting in a very light, low-contrast image just dark enough that the piece can still be read. The light image allows me to add color without the dark printed image bleeding through. This is why a light-colored wood is preferable to a dark wood.

34. I like a cotton paper—something with some "tooth." The image from the computer is printed with an inkjet or laser printer. I work over the printed image with graphite and colored pencils. Coloring could also be done on a computer, but I prefer the look, feel, and ease of this method.

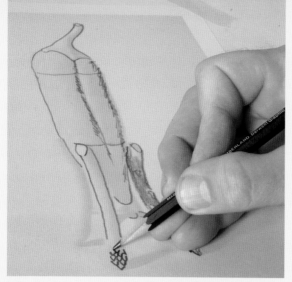

35. I fill in details such as the leaflets on the asparagus stalk and pulls. I may do many of these "studies" to try out different details.

The finished drawings are accurate in scale and perspective. I like that they are not too slick. I think this communicates the fact that there will probably be some changes in details when the actual piece is finished.

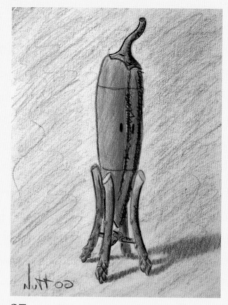

37. It is also easy to try out different color combinations while you are working on paper.

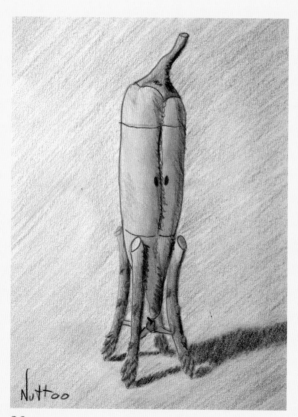

36. It is quick and easy to do other views.

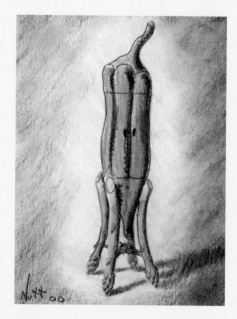

38. It was even easy to change the pepper to an okra pod. I might want to make this one, too—for someone in the South, no doubt.

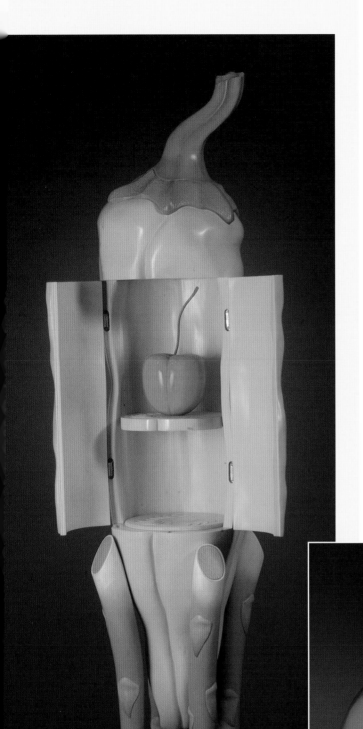

About the Artist

Craig Nutt found that he could talk with his Alabama neighbors about gardening, even when his early '70s appearance might have kept them away. When he went into business for himself, he lost the garden plot that his antique-shop employer had let him and his wife, Linda, use. Fantasizing about the beautiful vegetables he could have been growing, he decided to make a "flying vegetable" for a show of contemporary wind–animated art. "I thought someone should do it, and it was such a stupid idea that I figured I was the only person who would." Having made one piece, ideas for others began flooding his brain. Soon vegetables were becoming a vocabulary rich and flexible enough to convey what he wanted to say in his furniture. Rather than applying vegetation to a furniture part as he had done on period-style pieces, the orna-mentation was the structure, and that was a critical difference. Besides communicating through furni-ture and gardening, and teaching workshops at schools such as Penland, Nutt remains active in a number of organizations, including the Craft Emergency Relief Fund and The Furniture Society.

Gallery

Narrowing my list of artists to include in this section would have been doubly difficult if so many on my list had not been either writing chapters for this book or included in others' galleries. As far as I can tell, there is not a common aesthetic or technical thread that connects the work of these artists. Rather, each artist's work is unique, reflecting the intellect, experience, personality, and skills of that maker. Each artist creates works that are adventurous, yet each work is fully realized conceptually and skillfully wrought.

JOHN McNAUGHTON
Twisted House, 2005

13 x 8 x 8 feet
(4 x 2.4 x 2.4 m)
Cedar
PHOTO © ARTIST
COLLECTION OF THE INDIANAPOLIS ART CENTER, INDIANAPOLIS, IN

John McNaughton often takes a premise to its literal yet unexpected conclusion. If your life is turned upside down, is your house as well? His recent bark-veneered cabinets take furniture to its source and back again in a René-Magritte-meets-Art-Carpenter gambit.

Stephen Hogbin is the contemporary wood turner most responsible for demonstrating that the lathe can be used to generate nonconcentric forms if the turner visualizes cross sections, and then cuts apart and reassembles the turnings. Whether on an intimate or architectural scale, Stephen's work is marked by intellectual curiosity and an astute design sense.

Arthur Jones is a keen observer of nature and translates his observations into often delicate sculptures that recall skeletal forms, shells, and nature's latticework. Like a caterpillar that eats away the soft tissues of a leaf, leaving the lacelike veins, Arthur carves away more wood than one would think prudent or even possible to create form without weight. Yet the apparent fragility of the work belies its greater-than-expected strength.

Bob Trotman's figurative sculptures are as disconcerting as they are beautifully carved. Formerly a furniture maker, he uses furniture devices with a theatricality that intensifies the impact of his figures and makes you examine your own relationship to them. Drawers pull out of heads like core samples, a library ladder requires you to stand on a woman's back, and a magazine rack asks you to place your reading matter directly into a hollowed head.

Michelle Holzapfel combines intellectual domesticity, contemporary historicism, and a stone carver's sensibility as she releases objects from the burls she collects and stores in her "shedplex" in Vermont. She is often associated with the woodturning movement because many of her pieces begin life on her father's old metal turning lathe. But the objects are characterized by meticulous carving, which lends itself to the introspective nature of her work.

Kim Kelzer exploits her experience in pastry decoration and her quirky fashion sense in her exuberantly painted furniture. Typical of her brand of humor, she uses the disks from bathroom scales for the punched tin panels in her *Pie Safe*, implying the weighty consequences of cracking this particular safe.

Mark Sfirri is known for expanding a formerly obscure technique for making a turned approximation of a cabriole leg into a whole repertoire. The refinement and control he has brought to multi-axis turning is evident in the surprising synthesis of a caryatid and a cabriole leg in *Figurati*.

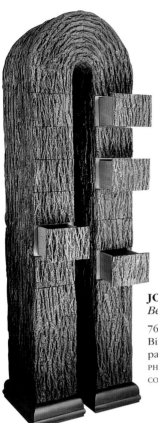

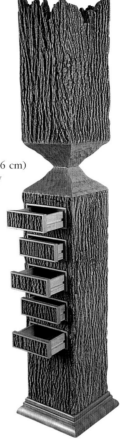

JOHN McNAUGHTON
Beaver Box, 2001

78 x 16 x 16 inches (198.1 x 40.6 x 40.6 cm)
Birch veneer plywood, ash bark, cherry
PHOTO © ARTIST
COURTESY OF CHAPMAN FRIEDMAN GALLERY

JOHN McNAUGHTON
Bent Tree, 2005

76 x 19 x 16 inches (193 x 48.3 x 40.6 cm)
Birch veneer plywood, ash bark, cherry, acrylic
paint; ebonized
PHOTO © ARTIST
COURTESY OF CHAPMAN FRIEDMAN GALLERY

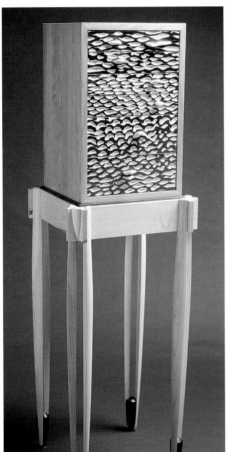

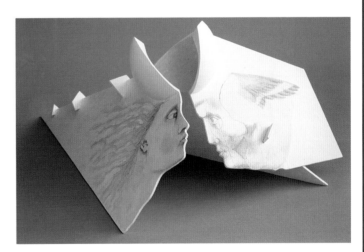

STEPHEN HOGBIN
Psyche & Mercury, 1990

10 x 23 x 16 inches (25.4 x 58.4 x 40.6 cm)
Wood, paint, graphite
PHOTO © ARTIST

STEPHEN HOGBIN
Formal & Loose Fragments, 2004

50½ x 15½ x 15½ inches (128.3 x 39.4 x 39.4 cm)
Cherry, maple, holly, paint
PHOTOS © ARTIST

ARTHUR JONES
Babel, 2002

23 x 12 x 10 inches (58.4 x 30.5 x 25.4 cm)
Fustic, matte acrylic, cotton cordage; carved
PHOTOS © ARTIST
PRIVATE COLLECTION

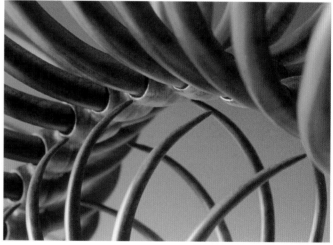

ARTHUR JONES
Nautilus, 2002

20 x 21 x 8½ inches (50.8 x 53.3 x 21.6 cm)
Black walnut, matte acrylic; sawn, carved
PHOTOS © ARTIST
PRIVATE COLLECTION

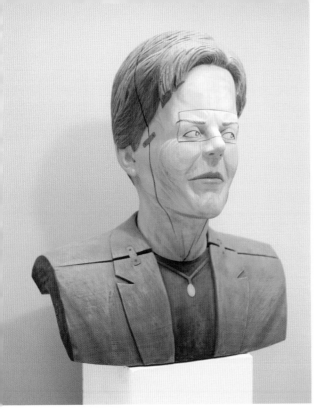

BOB TROTMAN
Lisa, 2005

29 x 26 x 20 inches (73.7 x 66 x 50.8 cm)
Poplar, steel, tempera, wax
PHOTO © ARTIST

MICHELLE HOLZAPFEL
Ingenue Vase, 2000

10 x 6 x 6 inches (25.4 x 15.2 x 15.2 cm)
Butternut, walnut; turned, carved
PHOTO © DAVID HOLZAPFEL
COLLECTION OF KENNETH SPITZBARD

MICHELLE HOLZAPFEL
Cushioned Bowl, 1998

7 x 14 x 14 inches (17.8 x 35.6 x 35.6 cm)
Maple (one piece); turned, carved, pyrography
PHOTOS © DAVID HOLZAPFEL

KIM KELZER
Pie Safe, 2001

58 x 21 x 18 inches (147.3 x 53.3 x 45.7 cm)
Mahogany, milk paint, tin from old bathroom scales,
old knobs; turned
PHOTOS © RACHEL OLSSON
COURTESY OF TERCERA GALLERY, PALO ALTO, CA

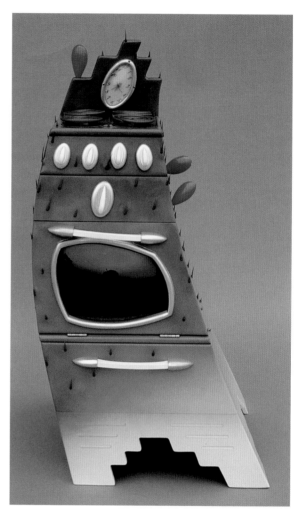

KIM KELZER
Home on the Range, 1993

36 x 22 x 20 inches (91.4 x 55.9 x 50.8 cm)
Wood, thermoplastic, aluminum, silicone, neon
PHOTO © ARTIST

KIM KELZER
Sit & Spin, Toilet Paper Holder with Rearview Mirror,
Magazine Holder, and Tampon Drawer, 2001

31 x 15 x 7 inches (78.7 x 38.1 x 17.8 cm)
Mahogany, plywood, milk paint, glass, found objects;
turned, assembled, mosaicked
PHOTO © RACHEL OLSSON
COURTESY OF GALLERY NAGA, BOSTON, MA

MARK SFIRRI and **AMY FORSYTH**
Figurati, 2003

54 x 24 x 17 inches (137.2 x 61 x 43.2 cm)
Walnut, paint; multi-axis turning on legs
PHOTO © JOHN CARLANO

MARK SFIRRI
"Slate" Bench, 2005

18 x 71 x 20 inches (45.7 x 180.3 x 50.8 cm)
Mahogany, paint; turned, carved
PHOTO © JOHN CARLANO

Craig Nutt

Paul M. Sasso

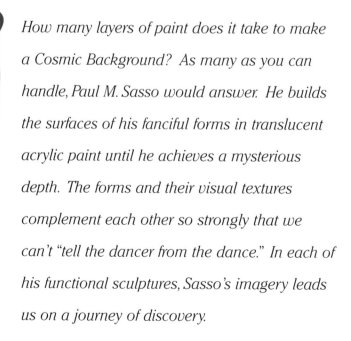

How many layers of paint does it take to make a Cosmic Background? As many as you can handle, Paul M. Sasso would answer. He builds the surfaces of his fanciful forms in translucent acrylic paint until he achieves a mysterious depth. The forms and their visual textures complement each other so strongly that we can't "tell the dancer from the dance." In each of his functional sculptures, Sasso's imagery leads us on a journey of discovery.

PAUL M. SASSO
Cosmic Background Explorer:
Are You on the Level?, 2004

95 x 37½ x 17¾ inches
(241.3 x 95.3 x 45.1 cm)
Acrylic on basswood, poplar,
gold leaf, maple, ebony,
clockworks

Cosmic Background Explorer

It started out innocently enough. It was really only dabbling in the taboo. It was backseat exploration. The year was 1977, and at the time nobody was supposed to do it. It was sacrilege, and to delve into it brought great scorn. It wasn't until a year later that I truly lost my virginity by accepting the idea of painting on wood, and for me there was no turning back.

In art school at that time there existed a great schism between the makers of "round art" and "flat art." This was good-humored for the most part, but it was real. One thing that both camps could agree on was that "craft" was as low as you could go—there was no place in the big A-R-T world for craft. Sneering was mandatory. My dilemma was that I loved it all. I could paint and draw, I could make sculpture, and amidst derogatory sniping from my fellow art students, I liked to make well-crafted furniture. Fortunately I was taken under the wing of my friend and mentor, William C. Law, who supported all of my harebrained ideas. Wood became my material of choice. I liked the directness of wood—you work it and it is done. Wood, however, is considered by the art world to be an inferior material, a prejudice I still don't understand. I didn't know a lot about the craft world during this period—but when I started to research it, I found that just as many exclusionary opinions also drove it. Battle lines were drawn everywhere I looked. Freethinkers need not apply!

My argument at that time and now is that the creative process all comes from a singular place—a place of intelligence and of the heart, a place where all things are possible. As far as I am concerned, whatever form, in whatever material, that emerges from a true and honest creative process is valid.

PAUL M. SASSO
Fuel, 2001
18 x 8½ x 6 inches (45.7 x 21.6 x 15.2 cm)
Acrylic and gold leaf on basswood and maple

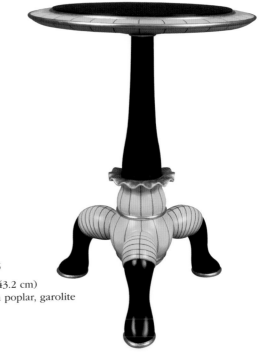

PAUL M. SASSO
Lil' Yellow Table, 2005
23¼ x 17 inches (59 x 43.2 cm)
Acrylic and gold leaf on poplar, garolite

I found my solace in museums, history being the great leveler of ideas. In museums you can mix and match, and compare and contrast; you can leap through centuries in a single day. I am still amazed when I look at artifacts from past human endeavors, always with an exclamation of, "Wow, somebody made all this stuff!" The great thing about being a maker of things is that you experience a deep connection with the makers of the past. All things truly are possible. Ideas are up for grabs. Freedom of thought is welcomed!

In 1978 I was in a little museum in Oberlin, Ohio, and was stunned by a 15th-century Italian carving of Saint Sebastian by an unknown maker. Here was an exquisitely carved and painted wood sculpture that embodied all of the things I admired most about art and craft. That statue altered my perception of my world. This was also the year I moved from Canada to the United States to attend graduate school at the University of Tennessee. I was going to study sculpture, but as it turned out, the university also had a wonderful painting department. I was welcomed in both. The marriage of wood sculpture and painting was a natural step in my development as an artist, and I had the encouragement and expertise of the faculty to guide me in my undertakings. I had found my artistic home.

As a new immigrant to the United States, I found that this country has a culture that screams, "Go big or stay home." I submerged myself in it as a wide-eyed child, and consequently this culture became the fodder for my work. Never out of ideas, I made a pledge to myself to make five paintings and one piece of

PAUL M. SASSO
Pink Belly, 2001

22½ x 12¾ x 6¼ inches (57.2 x 32.4 x 15.9 cm)
Acrylic and gold leaf on basswood and maple, glass, brass thermometer, lights

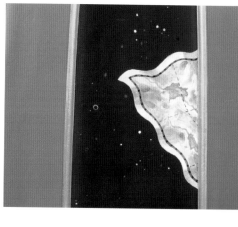

PAUL M. SASSO
The Zen of Mrs. Smart, 1997

82½ x 23 x 16 inches
(209.6 x 58.4 x 40.6 cm)
Acrylic on poplar, basswood, and maple, clock movement

PAUL M. SASSO

Decorative Arts #3—Italian Candy, 1996

66 x 16 x 16 inches (167.6 x 40.6 x 40.6 cm)
Wood, acrylic paint, clock movement

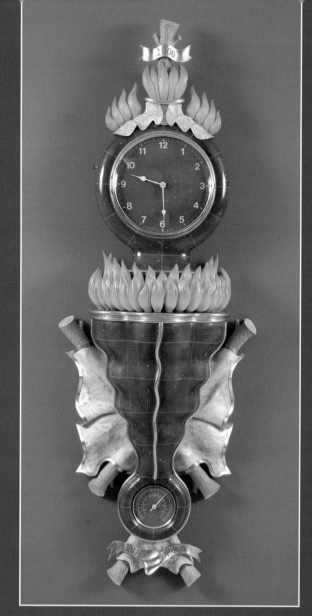

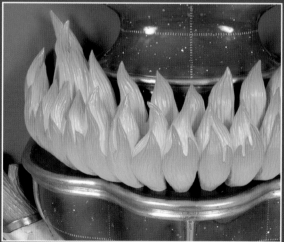

PAUL M. SASSO

New Era, 2000

57 x 20¼ x 8 inches (144.8 x 51.4 x 20.3 cm)
Acrylic and gold leaf on poplar, basswood, aluminum,
clock movement, thermometer, glass, brass

PAUL M. SASSO
Decorative Arts #2—Greco/Roman Happy Meal, 1996
69 x 20 x 15½ inches (175.3 x 50.8 x 39.4 x cm)
Wood, acrylic paint, clock movement

sculpture a week. I produced a lot of work. Sleeping was for sissies. I was supporting myself by making furniture and selling work to faculty members. Eventually the lines between painting, sculpture, and furniture became blurred, and the results of this merger became my life's work—"Go big or stay home!"

To help you better understand how my work evolves, let me take you on the journey of my influences and the thinking process involved in making a piece: *Cosmic Background Explorer: Are You on the Level?* (See page 41.)

I always begin with a premise that's fueled by my curiosity about the world. Research and the conclusions reached from this exploration set the stage for my art making. I began this clock after returning from a trip to Italy in 2002. The forms that particularly intrigued me in Italy were the shrinelike structures that celebrated the Madonna and had as their central focus a water feature, almost always a font of some sort. These structures had human proportions on a very large scale, like a giant mama! I felt that this format—a glorious combination of painting, sculpture, and function— was an ideal form to express my own demented view of the world.

The Premise

As an artist I have a tendency to look for the metaphorical value in all things. I came across an illustration for a water level (see below).

Water will always seek its own level, and builders have long used this simple principle to lay out buildings and gardens. For me the water level represents the gut metaphysics of moral exploration and subsequent action, the question being, "Are you on the level?" I had found my water feature.

PACKAGE IMAGE USED WITH PERMISSION OF
JOHNSON LEVEL & FULLER TOOL

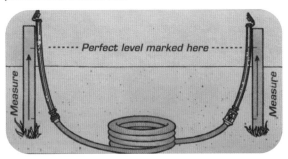

Because the water level indicated an internal value, I decided that the form to contain it would have to be representative of the external—the universe I live in. For this I turned to science. In 1989, NASA sent up a space probe to investigate the origins of the universe. It was called the "Cosmic Background Explorer." I particularly loved this name because in my own artistic way of discovery, I felt that I was a cosmic background explorer. The methods of artists and scientists may be different but the answers they seek are the same.

The Cosmic Background Explorer investigations proved that the faint uniform radiation emanating from deep space was generated by the "Big Bang." A subsequent satellite, launched in 2001 and called the "Wilkinson Microwave Anisotropy Probe" (WMAP), measured the temperature patterns and differences in the received microwaves. With this evidence scientists were able to assemble what has been referred to as a "Baby Picture" of the universe that was generated only 380,000 years after the Big Bang.

While studying the visual material on this subject, I was struck by the beauty of the patterns within the mapping of the scientific data. I decided that the coloration and the graphic lines of the mapping would be the basis of my clock. I found the shapes to be very womb-like and this fit

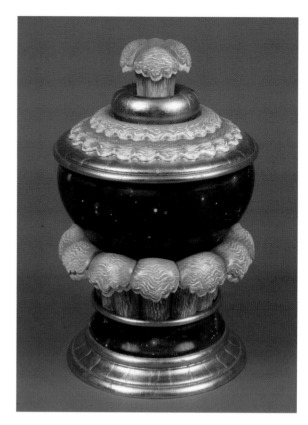

PAUL M. SASSO
Cosmic Background Explorer: Wavelength, 2003

13 x 8¼ inches (33 x 21 cm)
Acrylic and gold leaf on basswood and maple

Baby Picture of the Universe
COURTESY NASA AND WMAP SCIENCE TEAM

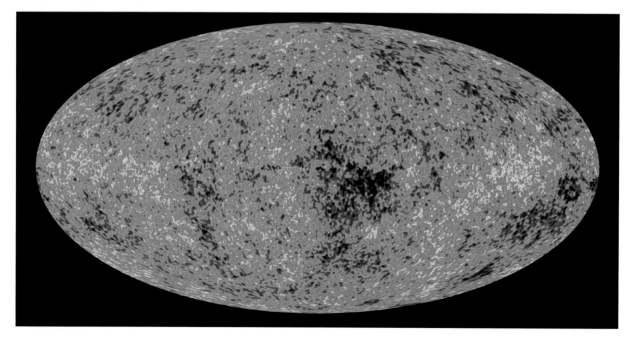

Paul M. Sasso

perfectly within the context of my "Big Mama." Its origins may be the language of science, but the metaphysical implications are for all of us.

Once the premise of a new piece is established, I begin by building a single element. In this case I carved and assembled the water level. I rarely plan the things I make, but instead build by reaction to a given element—here, the water level. Serendipity is a big part of my work method. I spend a great deal of time running scenarios through my head with the constant question "What if?" in mind. I make lots of drawings. Once a solution is reached, I have the daunting task of building it. What I do is not technically easy. For the most part it is a "rub your head and pat your belly while tap dancing" situation, but I like a good challenge. This free-for-all is the big fun! It's a balancing act between logic and intuition—a full brain activity. I have great respect for the tradition of woodworking methods, and I build within that tradition—I build to last. I decided that the water level should be enshrined in an enclosure that would have the spatial element of a night sky, giving the water level an illusionary size context. I also wanted to include a drawer under it; after all, this is a piece of furniture.

I have a particular fondness for curly maple, and almost all of the interiors of my functional pieces are made from it. The inlaid lines on the drawer bottom are ebony. I call this "fancy" work. Because of the enormity of this piece (it's almost 8 feet tall), I built the clock to come apart in three sections for easy moving. So working with the center section (the enshrined water level and the drawer), I set out to build a suitable base and the top section that would contain the clockworks.

Because my forms are complex, I use a whole array of technical methods to make them a reality: joinery, bending, laminating, turning, carving, and shaping—all very time-consuming. I build the bottom and top sections simultaneously. Because I teach, I have to manage my studio time in such a way that something is always getting done. I am very disciplined and dedicate five hours a day to studio activity. So, for example, while something is glued and drying, I will turn and carve some other element. As the pieces of the big puzzle are completed, I prop them up together so that I can gauge the relationships and proportions of the

PAUL M. SASSO
Cosmic Background Explorer: Are You on the Level?, detail

parts. I am not very mathematical when it comes to proportions, but instead rely on gut instincts. We have a saying around my house about aesthetic decisions: "It looks good, or it don't look good." Working in this way is always an adventure—action and reaction—it's artistic physics! This organic way of working gives the work personality and life.

Eventually the forms emerge out of this chaos, their formation simplified by keeping within the thematic scheme of the clock. Choosing the imagery has become easier because of a stylistic bag of tricks I have developed over the years. The basic elements of earth, air, fire, and water always show up in the work, and I always use a carved bead to define the forms. By "drawing" a line around everything, the forms become very tactile and understandable, like living on an island—you know your boundaries.

PAUL M. SASSO
Cosmic Background Explorer:
Are You on the Level?, details

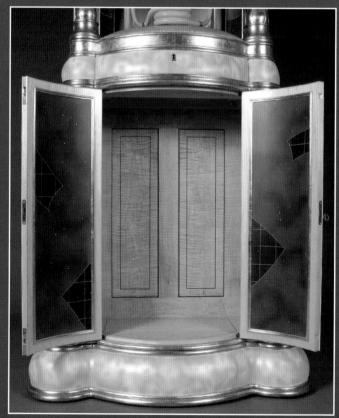

At this point the forms are "naked," but I am constantly aware that the raw wood surfaces will be painted. By running different scenarios through my head, I plot out my painting strategy. As the Hands On section of this chapter will show, I use a substantial amount of paint to achieve my surfaces. Most elements of the clock had to be painted before final assembly. Experience has taught me that paint has thickness that affects assembly. Careful masking of surfaces to be glued and building fixtures to hold the pieces for painting is an integral part of the process. Days of prep work are required, but this busy work gives me the opportunity to psych myself up for the actual painting. I have been painting for a long time and my sense of color is well entrenched in my brain; however, I methodically look for variation in color combinations to enhance my vision. The painting and gilding of the clock took weeks. After working on and off on this piece over a period of two years, *Cosmic Background Explorer, Are You on the Level?* was complete and all dressed up for the prom.

Art is not about materials and skills alone. Art is a cooperative relationship among materials, skills and the ideas that reflect and chronicle the time in which it is made. It is a whole-brain activity. Forms that emerge from art making, when this relationship is truly balanced, simply have a sense of wonder about them.

Only about four percent of the universe is composed of atoms—you and me and everything physical around us and that we know of. About 23 percent of the universe is "cold dark matter" which scientists know a little about, but a whopping 73 percent is "exotic dark energy," about which scientists know even less. Time and space have been a central component of my work for the past 30 years, and—as the above data demonstrates—there is ample opportunity for me to be a Cosmic Background Explorer!

Paul M. Sasso

Hands On

Paul M. Sasso introduces his technique of using multiple layers of transparent water-based paints to build surfaces that have visual depth of interest and meaning. Using this technique, endless possibilities emerge to push past the notion of paint as merely a coating on wood. By multiple layering, the builder can manipulate the surface with coatings that are sumptuous and reflect the intellectual substance of the maker's intent. He demonstrates this idea by painting a "star chart" of his own invention.

1. Meticulously preparing the wood surface is essential for any finish. I usually sand the wood with 220-grit sandpaper. Then I wet the surface with a sponge and, when it's dry, remove the raised grain with 320-grit sandpaper. I also prepare several panels to act as testing grounds. These panels are painted simultaneously with the real painting, thus keeping a record of the process. To begin the ground, a 1-inch or larger stiff white sable brush is wetted with water and dipped into the gesso. The trick here is to extend the amount of gesso on the brush to its maximum spreadability in one direction. This will be a very thin coat. This process is continued until all the surfaces are covered. When the first coat is dry, a second coat is applied at 90 degrees to the first coat. One more coat is

applied, again switching the direction of the brush strokes. Cross-brushing the gesso will develop a "tooth" on the surface for the paint to cling to.

2. A lot of medium and very little pigment are mixed for transparency. My formulas change depending on what effect I'm after, but I generally add only about one to two percent color to the medium.

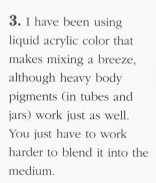

3. I have been using liquid acrylic color that makes mixing a breeze, although heavy body pigments (in tubes and jars) work just as well. You just have to work harder to blend it into the medium.

4. After a thorough blending, the mixture is poured and strained through cheesecloth into the spray-gun cup.

Paul M. Sasso

5. Painting the Star Chart: For an overview of the process, please refer to the sample panels at the end of this Hands On section (see page 46). I never start the painting process without extensive research into the concept I wish to convey. I study the reference materials, trying to grasp the essence of the image. I then rely on my own design sense and an informed eye to proceed.

6. For the Star Chart, I studied deep-space photographs and detected swirls of color in the picture plane. So the first colors that I sprayed on in a very random fashion were graffiti-like swirls. This will be the foundation and basic structure of the painting.

7. The whole picture plane is coated in its entirety with various transparent colors, letting each coat dry before adding additional colors.

8. After three coats of color are applied, the surface is wet sanded with 320-grit wet and dry sandpaper. "Sand-throughs" are inevitable and I welcome them, as they will add interest to the painted surface. This stage builds a basis for the following coats.

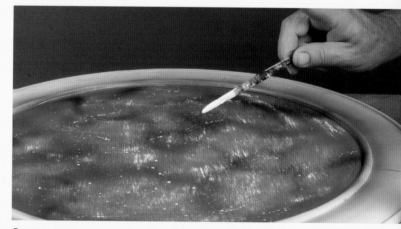

9. After sanding, a controlled splatter of titanium white dots (stars) is applied to the surface. These will eventually be very subtle but will add to the depth of the space scene. The same layering of color and dots is repeated (five more applications), and then a very heavy coat of clear gloss medium is applied. At this point a substantial amount of paint has been applied, and the painting should dry overnight to allow the paint film to "pull down."

The next morning the surface can be wet sanded with 600-grit paper to flatten it and to remove small imperfections caused by the dust particles and uneven paint buildup. The painting has now developed enough to add specific imagery.

Paul M. Sasso

10. For the Star Chart I have decided to add star clusters like those in the Milky Way. The entire surface is covered first with blue painter's tape, which does not leave adhesive on the painting when it's removed.

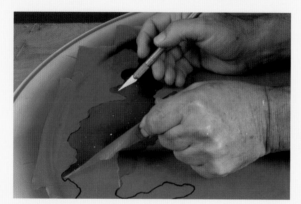

11. I draw the shapes I want with a marker; then the stencil is cut with a knife…

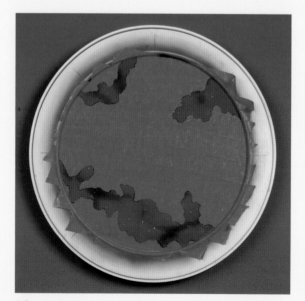

12. …and the excess tape is removed.

13. A heavy splatter of white dots is applied to the stenciled area. In some of my work I use this same technique to apply specific opaque shapes by spraying on titanium white and then hand-painting that shape. (See, for example, the map detail on *The Zen of Mrs. Smart* on page 35.)

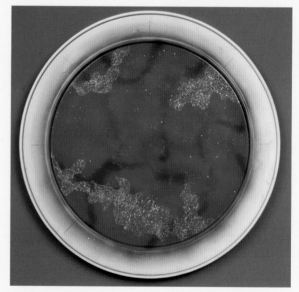

14. Once I am satisfied with the dot application, I remove the tape stencil. Then a heavy coat of transparent color is laid down (in this case Phthalo blue). When this heavy coat of paint dries, the surface gets wet sanded again with 600 grit. This sanding step has two functions: first, it modulates the surface, letting some of the color of undercoats come through; and, second, it leaves a slight tooth on the surface to allow for an easier application of the graphic materials used to complete the painting. The painting at this point has visual depth. Now is the time to add the icing!

15. I use a variety of graphic materials and tools to add detail to the painting. These include waterproof inks applied with compass and pens, as well as gel pens, vinyl tapes, letters, and numbers. If it leaves a mark on the surface, I use it.

17. Confidence, conviction, and a wet paper towel at hand to correct screwups is the way to go!

16. I always do test runs of my imagery on the test panels I have prepared. Here I am shown drawing different graphic details with ink and gel pens.

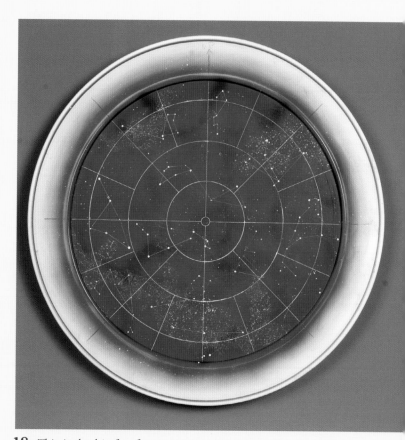

18. This is the big fun for me—inventing my own universe. On this piece I framed the imagery by applying imitation gold leaf on a coat of opaque matte red acrylic that substitutes for traditional red bole.

Paul M. Sasso

Sample Panels   All listed colors are mixed transparencies unless otherwise noted.

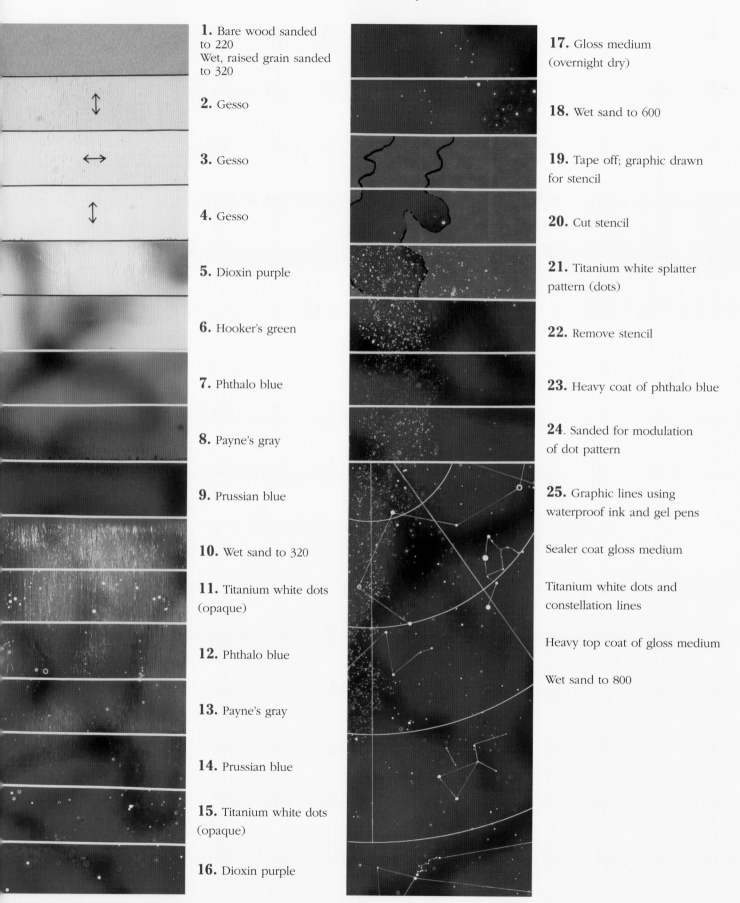

1. Bare wood sanded to 220
Wet, raised grain sanded to 320

2. Gesso

3. Gesso

4. Gesso

5. Dioxin purple

6. Hooker's green

7. Phthalo blue

8. Payne's gray

9. Prussian blue

10. Wet sand to 320

11. Titanium white dots (opaque)

12. Phthalo blue

13. Payne's gray

14. Prussian blue

15. Titanium white dots (opaque)

16. Dioxin purple

17. Gloss medium (overnight dry)

18. Wet sand to 600

19. Tape off; graphic drawn for stencil

20. Cut stencil

21. Titanium white splatter pattern (dots)

22. Remove stencil

23. Heavy coat of phthalo blue

24. Sanded for modulation of dot pattern

25. Graphic lines using waterproof ink and gel pens

Sealer coat gloss medium

Titanium white dots and constellation lines

Heavy top coat of gloss medium

Wet sand to 800

Paul M. Sasso

About the Artist

Paul M. Sasso was born in Canada, the son of a mason and a semiprofessional bowler. He spent a great portion of his childhood making things and daydreaming. He flunked out of high school because of the daydreaming. After working in the auto industry for four years, he was able to weasel his way into art school at the University of Windsor in his hometown. He embarked on many adventures including a two-year stint of living off the grid in northern Ontario, where he learned that self-reliance is disciplined hard work. He also grew to really appreciate electricity! In 1978 he moved to the United States to attend graduate school at the University of Tennessee in Knoxville. He graduated in 1981 with an M.F.A. in sculpture and began teaching woodworking and design at Murray State University in Kentucky, where he continues to teach today. During the summer, he often teaches at Penland. Sasso has received several awards for teaching excellence at Murray State. His work has been acquired by many important collectors and museums, including the Museum of Fine Arts in Boston, The Kemper Museum of Contemporary Art in Kansas City, and the Gulf Coast Museum of Art, in Largo, Florida.

Paul and his wife, Sandy, a painter, live and work at Sassoville, a compound of their own design and construction, near Almo, Kentucky, where they are surrounded by trees and other people's coon dogs. They share a love for late Gothic and early Renaissance art, Italian food, and travel. They could do without the coon dogs.

Gallery

I have always admired the work of those makers who approach their work with a sense of purpose beyond the marketplace. It is a difficult path to take. My selections for this gallery are based on my belief that one should always stay true to that little voice that drove us at the start and continues to steer us on our way. That little individual voice is the soul of our craft, the soul of our society. It defines what artists are and do. It has the capacity to make us happy! The work of these artists reveals a quality or feeling of both surface and form that to my mind is just right—a Goldilocks situation.

Stephan Goetschius is a maker of disciplined patience. His mandalas and shield figures are overwhelming in their superb execution, and at the same time, the work has a quiet presence that makes the ethereal visible.

Elizabeth Alexander is from what I call the "glue and grind" school of construction. What her work lacks in craft finesse is well made up for in sheer energy. Her painted surfaces, steeped in the history of painting, are a great catalyst for rumination. To view her work is to experience Elizabeth: crazy admirable comfort with relief from worldly woes.

Lanie Gannon's figures are a great reminder to us all that craft and concept can coexist beautifully. Her sculptural works are exquisite in their execution and simultaneously acknowledge a feeling of our everyday experience. We know these people, we can empathize with their situations, and she makes us conjure up from our own past an encounter with a familiar or similar person.

Travis Townsend's work is like a memento of when we were seven years old and still did things for all the right reasons—for the sheer joy of it—before we let things like mortgages and insurance payments pave our intentional way. The rawness of Travis's work helps us all get down to that place where we once began.

Michael Hosaluk is a reminder to those of us who fool around on the lathe that form does not have to follow a circle. With the added bonus of adding irreverence to the "twirler's" art, Mike expresses and shares his energy in a personal, hilarious way, thus proving one can be goofy and successful at the same time.

Simple luscious beauty! **Jo Stone**'s work is a great example of a rich and sumptuous marriage of idea, form, and technical ability. If woodworking were a fine wine, I'd drink Jo's work every evening.

STEPHAN GOETSCHIUS
Various Figures, 2004
Each, 28 x 4¼ x 1½ inches (71.1 x 10.8 x 3.8 cm)
Maple; burned, carved
PHOTO © TOM LABARBARA

STEPHAN GOETSCHIUS
Mandala 32, 2004

15 x 15 x 2 inches (38.1 x 38.1 x 5.1 cm)
Maple, 23-karat gold leaf; turned, burned, carved, gilded
PHOTOS © TOM LABARBARA

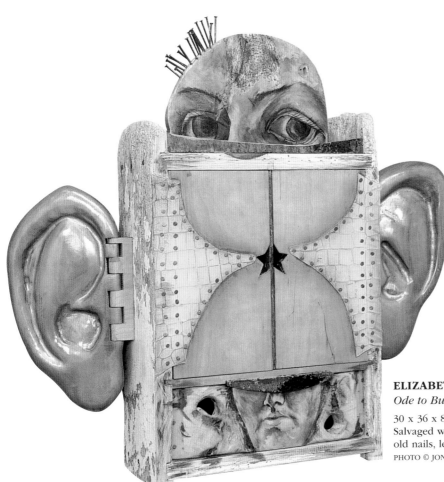

ELIZABETH ALEXANDER
Ode to Butthead, 2004

30 x 36 x 8 inches (76.2 x 91.4 x 20.3 cm)
Salvaged wood, cherry, poplar, pigment, tacks,
old nails, leather, tissue paper; assembled, carved
PHOTO © JON TAYLOR

Paul M. Sasso

ELIZABETH ALEXANDER
Nancy-Jane Day and the Tomato Farmer, 2005

55 x 48 x 18 inches (139.7 x 121.9 x 45.7 cm)
Walnut, pigment, tissue paper, tacks; carved,
constructed, burned
PHOTOS © ROBERT BATEY
COLLECTION OF ADELE POPE

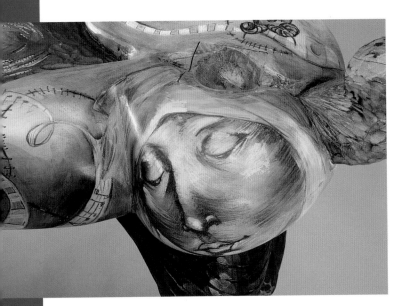

ELIZABETH ALEXANDER
Whores, Harems, and Wading Water, detail, 2003

18 x 50 x 15 inches (45.7 x 127 x 38.1 cm)
Poplar, pigment; carved
PHOTO © JAMES SCHUYLER
PRIVATE COLLECTION

ELIZABETH ALEXANDER
A Tennessee Vanity, 2005

15 x 18 x 9 inches (38.1 x 45.7 x 22.9 cm)
Poplar, pine, pigment, tacks, tissue paper; carved, burned
PHOTO © ROBERT BATEY
COLLECTION OF MERLE SMITH

Paul M. Sasso

LANIE GANNON
Mitrioshka, 2005

30 x 16 x 16 inches (76.2 x 40.6 x 40.6 cm)
Jelutong, acrylic paint; carved
PHOTO © ROBERT S. OGILVIE

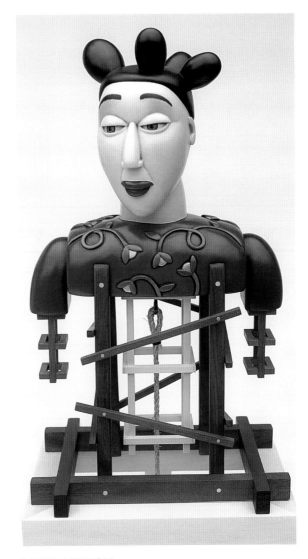

LANIE GANNON
Duomo, 2005

27 x 17 x 12 inches (68.6 x 43.2 x 30.5 cm)
Jelutong, mahogany, basswood, acrylic paint,
gold leaf, rope, metal hook; carved
PHOTO © ROBERT S. OGILVIE

LANIE GANNON
Francis, 2004

35 x 15 x 12 inches (88.9 x 38.1 x 30.5 cm)
Jelutong, acrylic paint, burlap; carved
PHOTO © KI OGILVIE

Paul M. Sasso

TRAVIS TOWNSEND
OXOXO Container/Toy, 2003

15 x 16 x 17 inches (38.1 x 40.6 x 43.2 cm)
Oak, basswood, cardboard, fabric, acrylic
paint, mixed media
PHOTO © MARY REZNY

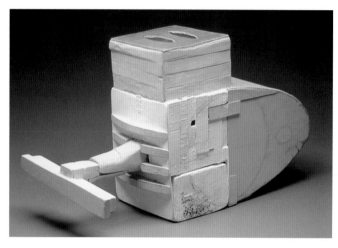

TRAVIS TOWNSEND
John's Device, 2000

14 x 24 x 12 inches (35.6 x 61 x 30.5 cm)
Poplar, maple, plywood, acrylic paint, mixed media
PHOTO © ARTIST
COLLECTION OF ROBERT PFANNEBECKER

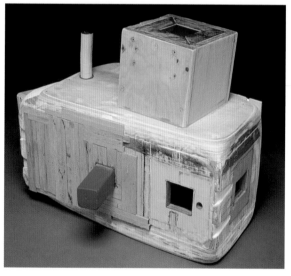

TRAVIS TOWNSEND
M.W.'s B.D. Toy, 2001–2003

19 x 27 x 16 inches (48.3 x 68.6 x 40.6 cm)
Plywood, poplar, acrylic paint, mixed media
PHOTO © TAYLOR DABNEY

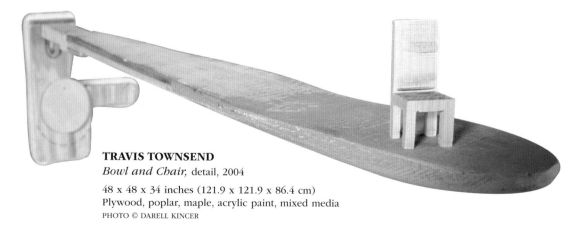

TRAVIS TOWNSEND
Bowl and Chair, detail, 2004

48 x 48 x 34 inches (121.9 x 121.9 x 86.4 cm)
Plywood, poplar, maple, acrylic paint, mixed media
PHOTO © DARELL KINCER

TRAVIS TOWNSEND

Framp's Processor, 2004

22 x 24 x 26 inches (55.9 x 61 x 66 cm)
Plywood, pine, maple, string, acrylic paint, mixed media
PHOTO © MARY REZNY

MICHAEL HOSALUK

Table, 2002

26 x 18 x 23 inches (66 x 45.7 x 58.4 cm)
Maple, acrylic paint, molding paste
PHOTO © GRANT KERNAN, AK PHOTO

MICHAEL HOSALUK

A Couple of Teapots, 2003

7 x 5 x 7 inches (17.8 x 12.7 x 17.8 cm)
Maple, acrylic paint, copper
PHOTO © GRANT KERNAN, AK PHOTO

Paul M. Sasso

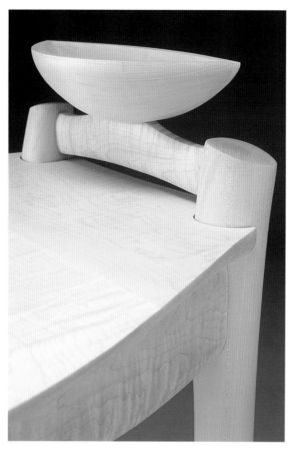

JO STONE

Entryway Table, detail, 2003

40 x 24 x 16 inches (101.6 x 61 x 40.6 cm)
Maple, curly maple, lacquer; mortise and tenon joinery,
dovetailed, carved
PHOTO © CHARLEY FRIEBERG

JO STONE

Plecoptera, 2003

22 x 14 x 3½ inches (55.9 x 35.6 x 8.9 cm)
Mahogany, paint; band saw box construction,
dovetailed, carved
PHOTO © UNIVERSITY OF NEW HAMPSHIRE PHOTOGRAPHIC SERVICES
PRIVATE COLLECTION

JO STONE

*Untitled (wall cabinet with
single drawer),* 1999

20 x 20 x 8 inches (50.8 x 50.8 x 20.3 cm)
Basswood, Swiss pear, milk paint,
natural finishes; dovetailed, carved, painted
PHOTO © RON PRETZER
PRIVATE COLLECTION

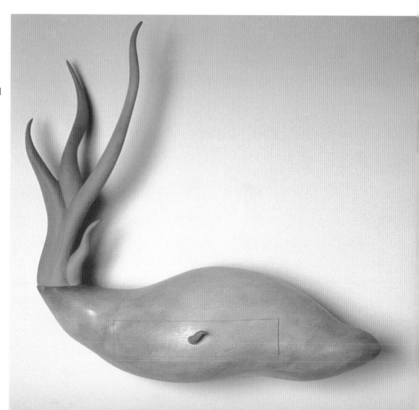

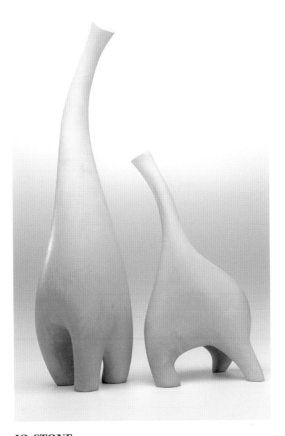

JO STONE

Wiggle 1 & Wiggle 2, 2004

Left, 11 x 3 x 3 inches (27.9 x 7.6 x 7.6 cm);
right, 7 x 4 x 4 inches (17.8 x 10.2 x 10.2 cm)
Jelutong; carved, painted
PHOTO © UNIVERSITY OF NEW HAMPSHIRE PHOTOGRAPHIC SERVICES
PRIVATE COLLECTIONS

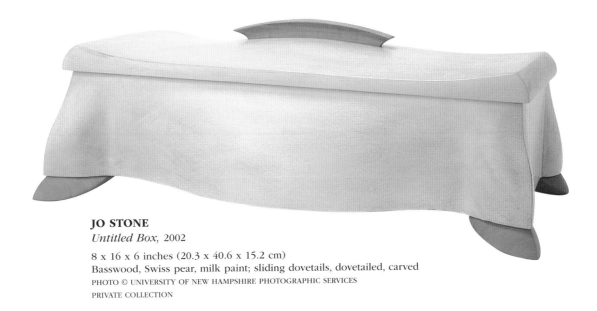

JO STONE

Untitled Box, 2002

8 x 16 x 6 inches (20.3 x 40.6 x 15.2 cm)
Basswood, Swiss pear, milk paint; sliding dovetails, dovetailed, carved
PHOTO © UNIVERSITY OF NEW HAMPSHIRE PHOTOGRAPHIC SERVICES
PRIVATE COLLECTION

Paul M. Sasso

Michael Puryear

After following a meandering path to studio furniture, self-taught Michael Puryear has found his forte. He aims to imbue his curvilinear work— inspired as much by cultural references as by functional concerns—with shibui, the Japanese sense of simple elegance. As difficult as it is to produce an elegant design solution, Michael has succeeded time and again. The curves in his furniture are often subtle, with just enough movement to beckon us closer.

MICHAEL PURYEAR
Front, *Barrow Chair*, 2003; back, *Screen*, 1997

See pages 59 and 65 for full caption

PHOTO © JONATHAN BINZEN

The Soft-Focused Eye

I grew up in an environment where teaching yourself was a natural way to learn. The idea was so subliminal that it was only as an adult that I became aware of how remarkable it was. I don't remember my parents suggesting that you could not try something. This was reinforced by trips to museums and libraries, as well as by family outings. Seeing family, friends, and neighbors working on their houses and property added to this sensibility. Some of these people I consider mentors. I feel this partially explains the fact that all my siblings and I engage in some sort of creative activity.

My path to becoming a furniture maker was not a linear one. In fact, it was not a path I had planned on taking. The direction of my life is as much a consequence of serendipity as it is planning. Even though this apparent lack of focus concerned me early on, I've come to see it as being essential to my process. My lack of success in my first attempt at college taught me that what seemed like failure at the time was an opportunity to grow. Growing up black in American society has taught me the value of following an independent path. All of this has contributed to qualities that I feel are fundamental to what I do. I find that being open to possibility and having the ability to follow one's personal path are essential to a craftsperson.

As far as creative ideas are concerned, I feel that mine are the consequences of my curiosity about both the manufactured and natural worlds. I have found that paying particular attention to things that resonate with me has given me a creative vocabulary of forms with which to communicate. This process of observation has to be nonjudgmental. I have come to call this "looking with the soft-focused eye." It means not only observing the particular, but also the context in which things exist. We must avoid letting the names we give things isolate them from the matrix in which they exist.

MICHAEL PURYEAR
Buffet II, 2003
56 x 48 x 18 inches (142.2 x 121.9 x 45.7 cm)
Bubinga, wenge
PHOTO © ARTIST

Another aspect of the life of a craftsperson is the importance of making. I feel that the act of making is an integrating experience. I think that this is of particular importance in these times, when most of our experience is conditioned by fragmentation and alienation. The values and experience one gains in the act of making are special. The reverberations of creating with an open mind and a sense of practice are empowering. By practice I mean the act of doing for the experience, not just for the results. The integration that I refer to concerns not only process, but also a level of control over one's life. The lives of Wharton Esscherick and James Krenov were inspirational for me.

MICHAEL PURYEAR
Barrow Chair, 2003

27½ x 29 x 32 inches (69.9 x 73.7 x 81.3 cm)
Bubinga, leather
PHOTO © ARTIST

As a self-taught furniture maker, I developed skills by designing within my comfort zone and adding one element that would challenge me technically. I instinctively found curves attractive. After doing several pieces that had curves cut from a single piece of wood, I wanted to explore more complex and integrated forms. This led to explorations in bending wood. My first effort was bent lamination, glued up in a mold, which resulted in legs for a dining table. The result was quite exciting and the technique opened up a whole new area of design potential. Since then I have investigated steam bending as well as using patterns and hand tools to shape three-dimensional forms. I have found panel forming with a vacuum press particularly useful.

As designers we take our inspiration from the world around us—a rich multiplicity of forms both natural and man-made. Natural forms in particular are often curvilinear. I believe this creates in us an emotional response to curves. Who does

not find the lines of a well-designed boat, automobile, or sculpture appealing? Curved forms used sensitively can convey a feeling of relaxed calm or of dynamic motion. For me this reaction is quite strong. I found that actually working with curved elements, however, is more complex than it often appears. Curved planar forms present special difficulties. Traditionally such work was done by coopering or brickstacking. Coopering requires ripping boards at the appropriate angle for the curve you want and gluing them together. This results in a faceted shape that needs to be planed to a smooth curve. Brickstacking is a more brutal technique, but the resulting blank can be contoured to any form. After gluing blocks of wood with alternating seams, you can cut a planar curve and veneer it to cover the glue lines. The development of panel forming added a new tool to that arsenal.

The ability to form panels of various contours has been available to industry for some time. As early as the 1870s there were experiments with this process, an outgrowth of the development of plywood. In the 1920s, during the Modernist movement, some designers used it to produce the simplified designs characteristic of that time. One of these designers was Gerrit Rietveld, who in 1927 designed the Beugelstoel. However it was Alvar Aalto, the Finnish architect and designer, who explored the process and used it with great success in the *Hybrid* chair, the

MICHAEL PURYEAR
Sideboard, 1995

54 x 46 x 19 inches (137.2 x 116.8 x 48.3 cm)
Sapele, mahogany
PHOTO © SARAH WELLS

MICHAEL PURYEAR
Wobble Stool, 2004

12 inches (30.5 cm) x variable dimensions
Bubinga, leather, aluminum, air cylinder
PHOTO © ARTIST

Paimio armchair, and *Model 31* armchair, along with other designs. Charles and Ray Eames's designs in the '40s and '50s relied heavily on this process. Coincidentally, during the Second World War, boats and planes were built with this technique, and it continues to be used to build strong, lightweight hulls for wooden boats.

The technique of building contoured panels from cross-grain stacks of veneer offers design possibilities that cannot be achieved in other ways. This opens up a whole new vocabulary of shapes to the furniture maker. In effect, you are making plywood in the form you want. Good results can be achieved by using multiple-part molds and a mechanical press, but the complexity and size of these presses prohibit their use by the average woodworker. The development of the small vacuum press, however, has put this

process in the hands of the studio furniture maker. The introduction of bending plywood and other manufactured sheet materials such as "wiggle board" has made making curved panels even easier.

I first used vacuum pressure to clamp veneer to panels, using a homemade press. That went well, and the process started to excite me. My first effort with a curved panel was in making a folding screen consisting of two curved panels that, when hinged together, formed an S curve. This shape allows the screen to stand up, and the two panels nestle into each other when folded together. Since then I have used curved panels in many projects and still have not exhausted their potential.

The process always begins with the design. I feel that design should not be driven by technique. I determine whether to use a given process based on its ability to achieve the results I want. Doing it the other way around produces results that often look forced and contrived. Having said that, when a design requires a curved panel, the panel must be defined as a line, the cross section of the form. The full-scale drawing of that cross section becomes the master for making the form for the vacuum press and also for planning the joinery that will connect the panel with other elements.

The vacuum press is just one tool among many, of course, but it allows me to design with forms that I otherwise wouldn't be able to make. I can't imagine what I'd be making now without a vacuum bag and bending plywood.

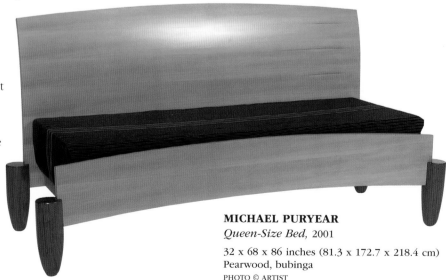

MICHAEL PURYEAR
Queen-Size Bed, 2001

32 x 68 x 86 inches (81.3 x 172.7 x 218.4 cm)
Pearwood, bubinga
PHOTO © ARTIST

Hands On

The curved planes in Michael Puryear's furniture are restrained, and their subtlety requires precise craftsmanship. Unfair curves and variations in lines would reveal themselves immediately, so the mold on which the plywood laminations are formed must be perfect. Michael demonstrates how he builds a large bending form and uses it to produce curved panels in a vacuum press.

1. Building the mold begins with laying out the curve for a pattern to make ribs for the bending form.

2. I cut the rib pattern on the band-saw.

3. Fairing the pattern. All the ribs will match this pattern, so anything wrong with the pattern will show up in the panel.

4. The ribs are sawn about ⅛ inch outside the line. Double-sided carpet tape is used to temporarily affix the pattern to each rib. Then the ribs get trimmed on a router table.

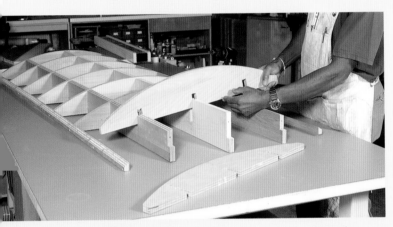

5. The ribs can be 5 inches apart, because the skin will be ⅝ inch thick. The rule of thumb calls for a 3-inch spacing with a ⅜-inch skin and a 6-inch spacing for a ¾-inch skin. After the slots are cut in the ribs and stringers, assembling the form can begin.

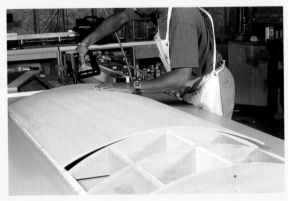

6. Nails and screws are used to apply the first skin layer of ⅜-inch wiggle board (bending plywood) to the form. The ends of the skin layers must land on the center of a rib.

7. Applying the second skin layer of ¼-inch melamine-coated fiberboard. The form will be used many times, and the melamine will resist glue sticking to it. This is an important step because there will be glue squeeze-out at the edges of the panel. Packing tape or paste wax can be used as a resist, too.

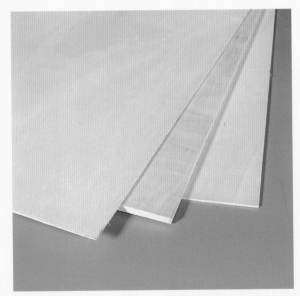

8. The three layers that will make up the finished ⅝-inch panel consist of one ⅜-inch wiggle board sandwiched between two layers of ⅛-inch bending poplar.

Michael Puryear

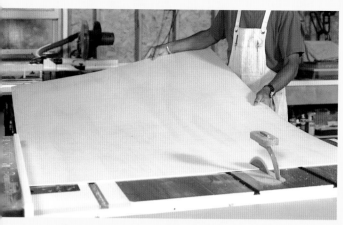

9. The table saw is used to cut the panels to size.

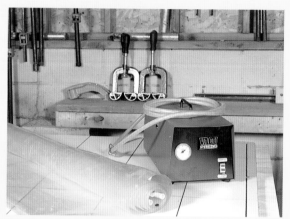

10. The vacuum press, consisting of the pump, hose, bag, and platen, is ready to go.

11. After making sure that everything is ready, the urea formaldehyde glue is mixed. I use a paint-mixing propeller driven by an electric drill. Avoid inhaling the dry powder.

12. A disposable foam roller cover is used to apply the glue. It puts down the correct amount of glue and produces a uniform film thickness. Glue should be spread on all faces that will be in contact with each other.

13. I secure the layers together at the center of each end. It is important that this be done only at the center to allow the panels to slip in the press. Screws, nails, staples, and tape all work fine.

14. Registration marks should be noted on the form and the panel so that the panel can be returned to the same position on the form for the veneering phase.

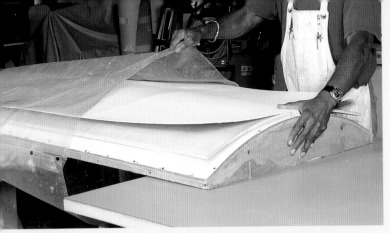

15. The press is loaded. The mold should be centered in the bag.

16. While the vacuum pressure builds, I'm pushing down on the panels while pulling out on the bag to make sure that the bag does not get sucked between the panels and the form.

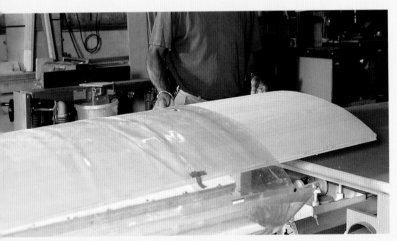

17. When the glue has cured, the press can be unloaded carefully to avoid cutting the bag with sharp glue squeeze-out. Veneering is the same as laying up the panel, except that the glue is applied

to both sides of the panel but not to the veneer. It would curl from the moisture in the glue and be impossible to handle. The registration marks must line up. This ensures that the panel is on the form exactly as it was when being glued up, and it prevents bubbles that may occur if the fit is not exact.

18. The curved edge of the panel is trimmed, using the form to guide a flush trim bit in the router.

19. The long edges can be trimmed on the table saw, using the form as a sled.

Michael Puryear

About the Artist

Michael Puryear, the third oldest in a family of seven children, was born in Washington, D.C., in 1944. After serving in the Army Medical Corps, he graduated from Howard University with a B.A. in Anthropology. He also worked 11 years for the D.C. Public Library. He moved to New York in 1974, where he worked as a freelance photographer.

A chance opportunity to do a kitchen renovation led to a brownstone renovation business. Dissatisfaction with the rigors of running a growing enterprise led to his moving into his shop to do cabinetry. Following his natural interest in design, he evolved into a studio furniture maker.

Michael's natural teaching ability has been demonstrated at most of the top craft schools around the country, including Penland. He has taught at Parson's School of Design and is currently an adjunct instructor at SUNY Purchase.

His work has been shown in galleries and museums nationally. Recently his work was included in "Studio Furniture: Expression & Function" at Emory & Henry College in Emory, Virginia. His work has been published widely, including in *Objects for Use: Handmade by Design*, published by Abrams. Michael's work is represented in several prominent collections, including those of the Cooper–Hewitt National Design Museum of the Smithsonian Institution, the African-American Design Archive, the Geraldine R. Dodge Foundation, Agnes Gund, Nancy Drysdale, and Rockefeller University.

He was honored in 2005 to be selected to deliver the Fiske Memorial Lecture at the Northeastern Woodworkers Association. In 2006 he was a Niche Award finalist and received a New York Foundation for the Arts grant.

MICHAEL PURYEAR
Screen, 1997
69 x 59 x ⅝ inches (175.3 x 149.9 x 1.6 cm)
Ash; dyed, filled
PHOTOS © SARAH WELLS

Gallery

The makers in this gallery represent a wide spectrum of styles, yet all of them use panel forming. In some pieces the technique is obvious, in others it is used more subtly. In all cases the makers use this process to achieve forms that are either impossible or impractical by any other method. As diverse as they are, they illustrate just some of the expressive potential of the panel-forming technique.

The *Lateen Chair* by **Janice C. Smith** expresses the dynamism and lightness that its name suggests.

Andrew Muggleton uses panel forming often and to great advantage in his work. The way in which his forms interact is very much part of their appeal; his *Balustrade Chaise* and *Arched Coffee Table* are good examples.

John Dodd's series of room dividers stress verticality. Through the use of wavy ribbons of wood he has introduced a curved element that contrasts quite successfully with the straight lines in the pieces.

The *Ribbon Chair* and *Bird Table* by **Richard Judd** share a calligraphic quality that animates them. They look as if their line were the flourish of a pen stroke that, given a third dimension, settles down and becomes functional form.

The work of **Mason F. Rapaport** often contains repeated curved elements, some changing in thickness throughout the form. This adds weight and interest to pieces such as *Coffee Table* and *End Tables*.

Bureau, by **Evan Hughes**, and *Side Table/Cabinets*, by **Robert Diemert**, both demonstrate a refined formalism that is enhanced by the choice of veneers.

The formed panel is not the first thing that strikes you about the work of **Mark Del Guidice**. His use of color and marking is the signature of his work, but the subtle use of formed panels, as in *Time's Up* and *Love Chest*, only adds to their uniqueness.

The interplay of forged steel and wood has become the signature of **Rob Hare**'s work, both materials contributing equally to the pieces. By using curved panels, he has been able to integrate these materials very successfully. In *Bowed Drop-Front Desk* and *Bed with Bedside Table*, the visual weight of the pieces comes from the wooden elements—the reverse of our expectations.

The *Guitar Series* of chairs by **Marian Yasuda** displays Picasso-like imagery and shows that a set of chairs does not have to be a carbon copy of each.

JANICE C. SMITH
Lateen Chair, 1995

38 x 66 x 24 inches (96.5 x 167.6 x 61 cm)
Plywood with sapele pommele veneer, upholstery; knock-down construction, formed plywood seat, torsion-box construction
PHOTOS © REUBEN WADE

ANDREW MUGGLETON
Balustrade Chaise, 2002

29 x 59 x 20 inches (73.7 x 149.9 x 50.8 cm)
Wenge, mahogany, aluminum, Ultrasuede; bent lamination
PHOTO © DEAN POWELL

ANDREW MUGGLETON
Arched Coffee Table, 2003

16 x 45 x 35 inches (40.6 x 114.3 x 88.9 cm)
Bubinga, wenge, stainless steel, glass; bent lamination
PHOTO © DEAN POWELL

JOHN DODD
Room Divider I, 1988

80 x 36 x 18 inches
(203.2 x 91.4 x 45.7 cm)
Walnut, bee's wing narra, slats, small table;
curved, laminated
PHOTO © WOODY PACKARD

JOHN DODD
Room Divider II, 1988

80 x 48 x 22 inches
(203.2 x 121.9 x 55.9 cm)
Ash, anigre, machiche; curved, laminated
PHOTO © WOODY PACKARD

JOHN DODD
Room Divider IV, 1990

72 x 36 x 16 inches
(182.9 x 91.4 x 40.6 cm)
Cherry, anigre, wenge; curved, laminated
PHOTO © WOODY PACKARD

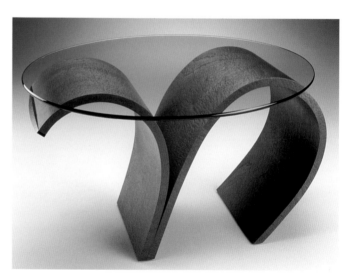

RICHARD JUDD
Ribbon Chair, 2002

30 x 20 x 36 inches (76.2 x 50.8 x 91.4 cm)
Kewazinga, birch bending ply, varnish; vacuum formed
PHOTO © WILLIAM LEMKE

RICHARD JUDD
Bird Table, 2001

22 x 36 x 30 inches (55.9 x 91.4 x 76.2 cm)
Sapele, birch bending ply, wenge, glass; vacuum formed
PHOTO © WILLIAM LEMKE

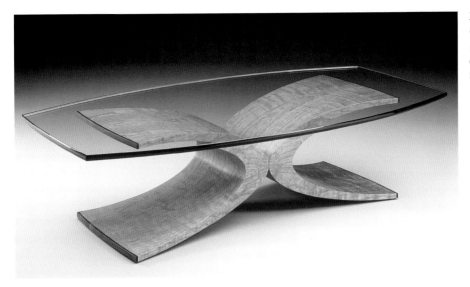

MASON F. RAPAPORT
Coffee Table

15 x 60 x 30 inches (38.1 x 152.4 x 76.2 cm)
Cherry, walnut; figured
PHOTO © DEAN POWELL

MASON F. RAPAPORT
End Tables

Each, 23 x 24 x 24 inches
(58.4 x 61 x 61 cm)
Cherry, walnut; figured
PHOTO © DEAN POWELL

EVAN HUGHES STUDIO
Bureau, 1998

32 x 81 x 23 inches
(81.3 x 205.7 x 58.4 cm)
Satinwood, maple, steel
PHOTO © LYDIA GOULD

ROBERT DIEMERT
Side Table/Cabinets, 1995

Each, 20 x 22 x 22 inches (50.8 x 55.9 x 55.9 cm)
Bubinga, ebony; carved
Photo © Jeremy Jones
CHALMERS COLLECTION

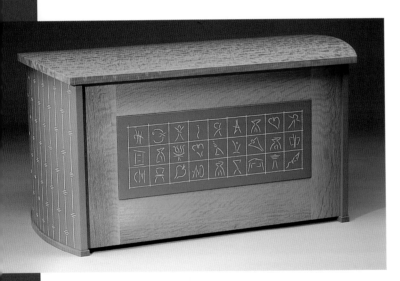

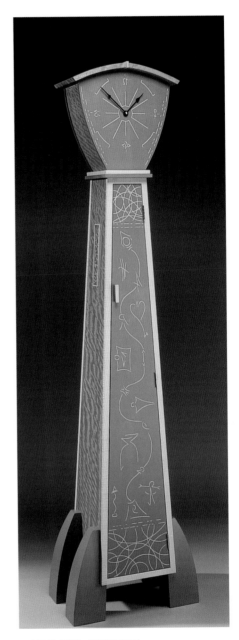

MARK DEL GUIDICE
Love Chest, 2005

21 x 40 x 21 inches (53.3 x 101.6 x 53.3 cm)
White oak, makore, basswood, MDF, milk paint;
carved, bent lamination
PHOTO © CLEMENTS/HOWCROFT

MARK DEL GUIDICE
Time's Up, 2004

80 x 21 x 14 inches (203.2 x 53.3 x 35.6 cm)
Bubinga veneer, curly maple, basswood,
milk paint, quartz movement, Italian poplar;
incise carved, bent lamination
PHOTO © CLEMENTS/HOWCROFT

ROB HARE

Bowed Drop-Front Desk, 2004

Closed, 48 x 44 x 22 inches (121.9 x 11.8 x 55.9 cm); open, 48 x 44 x 38 inches (121.9 x 11.8 x 96.5 cm)
Curly maple, forged steel; lacquered, vacuum formed
PHOTOS © CHRIS KENDALL

ROB HARE

Bed with Bedside Table, 2000

Bed headboard, 48 x 72 x 12 inches (121.9 x 182.9 x 30.5 cm); table, 24 x 20 x 16 inches (61 x 50.8 x 40.6 cm)
Cherry, steel, maple, claro walnut; figured, forged, lacquered, coopered, resawn, curved, laminated
PHOTO © CHRIS KENDALL
PRIVATE COLLECTION

MARIAN YASUDA

Guitar Series, 2003

Each, 39 x 29 x 28 inches (99.1 x 73.7 x 71.1 cm)
Koa, ebony, leather
PHOTO © JOHN DE MELLO
PRIVATE COLLECTION

Curtis Buchanan

A contrarian in the orthodox sphere of Windsor chair makers, Curtis Buchanan challenges us to look closely at his work, so that we realize only gradually how subtle alterations here and there combine to make a new and cohesive form. Although he says that designing Windsors is easy because the seat divides two areas that can be considered separately, his own chairs tell a different story.

CURTIS BUCHANAN
Comb-Back High Chair, 1988

34 x 18 x 18 inches (86.4 x 45.7 x 45.7 cm)
Maple, oak, pine, milk paint, oil

Keeping It Simple

My dad passed through the old barn, his eyes picking up not on what was there but what wasn't. The shoe last, the Civil War saddle, ten-gallon milk cans—all things that someone (namely my cousin) had taken. My grandfather had been dead for four years. The nine siblings had failed to get together and divide things up as they had promised. Now much of it had disappeared. He walked through the breezeway, under the scuttle hole to the hayloft and out the large double doors, where his eyes caught sight of the froe. It was large—1½ feet long, with a forge weld of at least 4 inches.

Froes were found on all southern Appalachian farmsteads. They were the workhorses of dimensioning tools. They split wood or, more precisely, rived it. Splitting boards is quicker than sawing and yields straight grain for strength and workability with a drawknife. Fence palings and roof boards were made by the thousands in the slow winter and laid by for later use. The split surface of chestnut and white oak didn't open up wood fibers, so water was shed with ease, and the roof or fence lasted a generation. This froe had been in the family for at least 100 years. He picked it up, ignoring his ingrained nature that would have prohibited such an act, and stepped out into the sunlight, never dreaming that this ancient tool would ever do any more than hang on a wall.

Tomorrow, as I have done for more than 20 years, I will pick up that froe and rive out chair parts. With each spindle, back, and leg I split, pieces with end-to-end grain vastly superior to any sawn board, I reconnect with my past.

My froe is my table saw. The spokeshave gently shapes and takes the place of sandpaper, and the versatile drawknife performs a myriad of tasks. The tools are chosen for reasons beyond their speed and accuracy; their feel in my hands, the sound made as a sharp blade severs wood fibers, and the fun of using them. It was the tools that led me to chair making and that continue to keep me there.

CURTIS BUCHANAN
Sack-Back Armchair, 1988

38 x 25 x 20 inches (96.5 x 63.5 x 50.8 cm)
Maple, oak, pine, milk paint
PHOTO © TOM PARDUE

They're user-friendly, quiet, and dust-free. The joy they cause starts with picking them up and feeling their smooth worn handles, and finishes with noiseless cuts. I've made thousands of spindles, yet sitting on my shaving horse and slicing through freshly cleaved oak with my drawknife still brings about a mesmerizing serenity.

As the years passed and my collection of hand tools grew, I began to plan for my most important

Curtis Buchanan

CURTIS BUCHANAN
Continuous Armchair,
detail, 2005

38 x 24 x 22 inches
(96.5 x 61 x 55.9 cm)
Maple, pine, oak, milk paint
PHOTO © FRESH AIR PHOTOGRAPHICS

CURTIS BUCHANAN
Clockwise from top right:
Comb-Back Chair, 2005, see bottom right for complete caption;
Stool, 2005, 25 inches (63.5 cm) tall, walnut, butternut;
Continuous Armchair, 2005, see top right for complete caption
PHOTO © FRESH AIR PHOTOGRAPHICS

CURTIS BUCHANAN
Comb-Back Chair, detail, 1989

45 x 27 x 23 inches (114.3 x 68.6 x 58.4 cm)
Oak, milk paint
PHOTO © FRESH AIR PHOTOGRAPHICS

CURTIS BUCHANAN
Writing Armchair, 1998

48 x 36 x 24 inches
(121.9 x 91.4 x 61 cm)
Maple, oak, pine, poplar,
milk paint, oil
PHOTO © PETER MONTANTI

supper I retire to my porch to sit for a while before going to bed. Sometimes I look out across the field, and I see that fellow plowing with his lights on.'"

As with all good stories, the lessons this one teaches are as different as the people who hear them. I have electricity and I'm glad I do. The lesson for me is protecting myself from myself. I very carefully weigh the decision of whether or not to add a new tool. What will its unseen repercussions be? Will it bring me closer to my work or create a greater separation? And if you ever see me working with my lights on, I hope it's because the sun hasn't come up.

My tool decisions have not all been as wise as those concerning my shop. Take my first steambox. I plunged into it with the desire to build a super box, but I had very little knowledge. I owned a propane tank that I felt should be sufficient to boil a couple of gallons of water. After a visit to a scrap metal yard, I owned an 8-inch x 8-foot length of pipe with ¼-inch-thick walls. I got a welder to cut

tool, my shop. I knew the site—my backyard—so my drive to work would be a 200-foot-long walk past flowers, tomatoes, and raspberries. I determined its size—16 x 20 feet—just large enough to keep organized. And I decided on its construction: post and beam—a righteous method for a righteous craft. What I couldn't decide was whether to install electricity. The answer came to me from an old, now deceased woodworker named Daniel O'Hagan.

Daniel listened quietly as I recounted my shop plans. I then mentioned my electricity dilemma. Daniel emitted a low "hmmm," and slowly said, "As you know, I live with Amish. I'm not Amish, but they let me live with them. One day a tractor salesman approached my neighbor and told him of all the advantages of a tractor: It takes less physical energy, you can plow more ground in a day, and it only eats when it works. My neighbor replied that he knew all about a tractor. The fellow across the field had one. He said, 'In the evening, after a day of plowing, I bring my horses into the barn. I give them feed and water, and I brush their coats. After

CURTIS BUCHANAN
Bird Cage Side Chair, 1993

37 x 19 x 18 inches (94 x 48.3 x 45.7 cm)
Maple, oak, pine, milk paint, oil
PHOTO © TOM PARDUE

CURTIS BUCHANAN
Loop-Back Chair, 1989

38 x 19 x 22 inches (96.5 x 48.3 x 55.9 cm)
Maple, oak, pine, milk paint
PHOTO © TOM PARDUE

hot plate, and—presto—a steambox I used for years. I let a few weeks pass before I sheepishly sold my now reconfigured 8-foot pipe back to the scrap metal yard and recouped less than one-twentieth of my original investment. Admitting the failure to my wife took a while longer.

My current steambox is an evolution of many years but is still very simple. The same can be said of my designs. Like my steambox that appears different but steams wood for bending as it always

CURTIS BUCHANAN
Velda's Chair, 2002

46 x 26 x 24 inches (116.8 x 66 x 61 cm)
Walnut, butternut, hickory, oil
PHOTO © PETER MONTANTI

2 feet off the pipe, cut a hole in the middle of the 6-foot-long section, and weld the 2-foot-long section over it, to create a "T." A plate was welded to the bottom of the "T" and a 1½-inch-diameter pipe was added to the side to add water. I finished it off with plates and gaskets clamped to the ends and a pressure relief valve so that dangerous steam pressure wouldn't build up, explode, and kill me. After $85 we didn't have, two days, three friends, and much justifying to my wife, I had created my first and only piece of nonfunctional sculpture—300 pounds of it. There was so much iron that a blast furnace couldn't have boiled the water. I quickly made a 1 x 1 x 6-foot snake coffin from scrap plywood, set it over a pot of water, set the pot on a

CURTIS BUCHANAN
Patra's Chair, 1992

39 x 22 x 19 inches (99.1 x 55.9 x 48.3 cm)
Maple, poplar, oak, milk paint, oil
PHOTO © PETER MONTANTI

has, my chair designs change within the Windsor style but, as before, keep you comfortably separated from the floor.

Designing within the Windsor style, a style that is defined by the fact that all parts stop at the seat, is unique. Because the parts stop at the seat (for example, the back legs do not continue up to form the back post), the chair maker has the advantage of designing below the seat independent of designing above it. In many chairs, the seat is the last element added. In Windsors the starting point has to be the seat—without it, all you have is a handful of sticks.

Patra's Chair (left) was developed using the seat of a fan-back side chair as a base. I kept the leg, post, and spindle mortises the same but removed the pommel and added angular corners to the front. I imagined the sitting area mimicking a different material, so I carved it to an almost puffy look and separated it from the rest of the chair with a groove. I further accented it by using a wadded-up paper towel to dab thick, black, milk paint over a red base.

With the seat done, I was ready to tackle the undercarriage. I wanted a light, uplifting appearance. To achieve this, I raised the stretchers up as high as structurally possible and tapered the legs below to a very small foot. The cove was added to separate the tapers going in opposite directions, to break up the monotony of the straight line and to give two crisp horizontal details. The idea for these changes came from a photograph I had seen long ago of a chair made by a man named Wes Lowe. It struck me hard at the time and stuck with me.

The most technically difficult element of the chair that I faced was the back. The shape of the spindles and post was easy: just continue the theme of the legs. The shape and bending of the crest was also straightforward, but for the juncture of the crest and post, I wanted a clean, angular joint mirroring the front of the seat. After mocking up several choices, I settled on a joint found in birdcage and rod-back Windsors of the late 18th and early 19th centuries—the false miter. However, I needed more strength than this round mortise and stub tenon could deliver. I ended up sawing a ¼ x ⅜ x ⅝-inch tenon and

chopping a matching rectangular mortise in the crest. The result was a joint that was plenty strong and a look that gave the false impression that the post continued on up to the top of the crest. In actuality, the post shoulders against the bottom of the crest, and the false miter is carved entirely into the crest itself.

I work within a tradition but attempt to move that tradition forward with small design changes. While I enjoy and savor the new challenges associated with design, my peace lies in the rhythm of repetition. The difference between being motivated by the end result and floating downstream with the process has been seen by many as the defining point between the artist and craftsman. Like all stereotyped ideals, this one is no closer to being reality than the reverse of itself.

I was reminded of this one summer day in Smithville, Tennessee. I was a presenter at a Furniture Society Conference and had walked down to my seminar room early, only to find it occupied. Sculptor Bob Trotman was showing how one could infinitely increase the size of a maquette using only a right triangle and a pair of calipers. It was a process that connected Bob with artists and craftsmen as far back as ancient Egypt. His excitement, as he crawled around on the floor, was obvious and was a reflection of his joy when immersed in this activity in his own studio. "Bob," a voice came from one of the onlookers, "you know you can do that on a computer." The simple response from a person who enjoys his work was "Why would I do in 30 minutes what I enjoy doing for four hours?"

Tomorrow, I will pick up my froe and connect and reconnect with every person who creates with his hands.

CURTIS BUCHANAN
Patra's Armchair, 1992

42 x 26 x 24 inches (106.7 x 66 x 61 cm)
Maple, oak, poplar, milk paint
PHOTO © DOUG THOMPSON

Hands On

Curtis Buchanan demonstrates how he assembles his Windsor chairs using the tools and methods he's found to work best. An antique Spofford brace and Cooke's patent augers, rubber bands, electric tools, and shop-made fixtures to hold particular pieces— all of them make the work go along smoothly and with comparative ease. Still, each chair is a singular endeavor, requiring that Curtis respond to the structure as he builds it rather than to any pattern.

1. The positions of the holes for the center spindle and the two front arm supports are laid out on the top of the seat. Then the center spindle hole is bored. This photo shows the old Spofford brace I use, which is much better balanced than more recent braces.

2. The arm support holes in the seat are cut next. To achieve the correct angle, I use an adjustable bevel and a square, one for each plane.

3. After the seat has been carved, the leg holes are bored from the top of the seat.

80 THE PENLAND BOOK OF WOODWORKING
Curtis Buchanan

4. All the holes in the seat get tapered. I use the same bevel system to fine-tune the angle. The taper reamer has a 6° included angle. Most chair makers use an 11° one, but I feel that 11° is too wide.

5. To measure the length of each stretcher, I insert the legs (dry) into the seat and, using a folding rule with an extension, measure shoulder to shoulder and add a 1⅛-inch tenon.

6. To measure the mortise angles for the side stretchers, I stretch rubber bands around all four legs at stretcher height. Then I can easily measure the angle by placing a protractor at the leg/rubber band intersection.

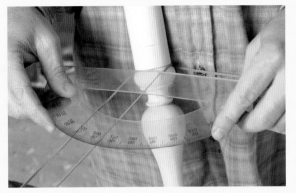

7. The mortise angles for the center stretchers are measured in the same way.

8. Then the stretcher holes are bored. The leg is held securely and leveled using a three-peg holding system with a wedge. With V-blocks on two pegs, the system automatically levels the leg. The mirror and the adjustable bevel help maintain the correct angles.

9. After gluing the mortises and tenons of the undercarriage, the parts are assembled quickly, stretchers first.

Curtis Buchanan

10. A very slightly over-sized, super-dried tenon is pounded into a mortise that is at equilibrium moisture content. The tenon will expand as it takes up moisture from the wood around it.

13. To determine the positions of the arm-support holes in the arm rail, a rubber band is stretched between the tops of the arm stumps, which are set dry in the seat. I measure from the center of the rubber band to the top of a dummy spindle placed in the center spindle hole. This measurement enables me to mark the arm-stump hole position in the handhold of the arm rail.

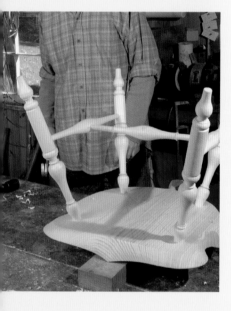

11. The leg tenons have been glued, and the legs have been pounded firmly into the tapered holes in the seat.

12. Glued wedges are pounded into the tenon ends until the hammer sound turns dead. Note that the slots in the tenons are sawn, so they run across the grain of the seat.

14. The measurement is transferred to the center of a straightedge squared with a large compass. Then the top of the arm gets marked because the measurement was taken at the tops of the arm-support tenons, and the holes should be bored from the top to avoid tearout there.

15. While referring to the adjustable bevel, the mortise holes are bored. The photograph above shows how deeply I carve the arms.

16. The holes for the arm supports get tapered from the bottom of the arm.

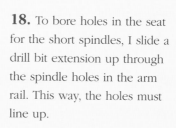

18. To bore holes in the seat for the short spindles, I slide a drill bit extension up through the spindle holes in the arm rail. This way, the holes must line up.

19. The holes in the arm for the long spindles are drilled from the top, again sighting at the corresponding spindle positions on the seat. Then the holes can be bored in the seat, using the drill extension to align the holes.

17. With the arm rail placed on the arm stumps, the spindle holes are bored in the arm rail. A support dummy is placed under the arm rail at the back of the seat to hold it at the correct height. This angle is achieved by sighting at the corresponding spindle position marked on the seat.

20. The long spindle holes in the arm rail are slightly tapered using a large rat-tail file. I chuck it in the bit brace and turn it counterclockwise.

Curtis Buchanan

21. The arm stumps, spindles, and arm rail on the seat are assembled without glue, keeping the arm rail horizontal.

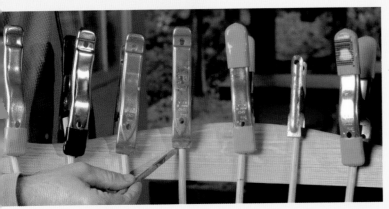

22. With the long spindles held in place by spring clamps, the spindles are traced on both sides to locate and align their holes in the comb. I splay the long spindles more than most makers, but they look just right to me.

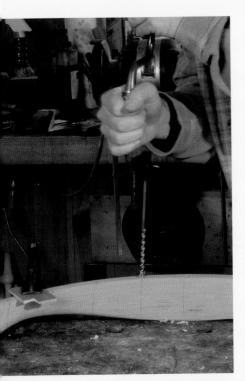

23. The comb is clamped upside down on the bench, so the holes can be drilled easily. They're centered on the edge of the comb and aligned with the spindle tracings.

24. The comb is placed on the spindles and leveled by measuring from the seat.

25. Now is the time to tweak every part above the seat—for example, rotating spindles to a clean fit, and making sure the arm rail is level and handholds are flat. When I'm satisfied, I mark the positions of every piece before disassembling the arms and back.

26. Gluing up and setting the parts follows a particular sequence: arm stumps in the seat, then short spindles in the seat, then long spindles in the seat, then arm rail on the spindles, and then the comb.

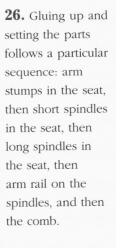

27. Wedges in the arm stumps and short spindles secure the arm in position.

28. To pin the comb 7/64-inch holes are bored through the outer spindles and the center one, then 7/64-inch square hickory pins are driven through the comb/spindle joint. The comb is backed up with a maul while the pins are set.

29. One final thing: I use a special kind of antique auger bit to bore many of the holes in my chairs. The bit on the left cuts very easily and can start a hole at any angle without tearing out. The auger is called, variously, a Cooke's patent, gedge, or scotch-eyed bit. This one is dated 1851. On the right is a standard contemporary bit.

About the Artist

Having "lit out" occasionally since he was 16, Curtis Buchanan hitchhiked his way through 48 states and 20 countries, and spent seven years in the 1970s just looking around and meeting people—more blasting through his horizons than expanding them. Then, during a stop back in Tennessee to make a little money, he became better acquainted with his future wife, Marilyn, and abruptly decided to stay put for a while. Soon enough, they decided to find a place to live and did so by driving around the countryside until Marilyn said, "This is it!" They live on Main Street in Jonesborough, Tennessee, within sight of the town hall and walking distance of the library. These days Curtis leaves primarily to conduct workshops at such venues as Penland School of Crafts.

"Living on the road got me hooked on freedom, so I looked for the same qualities in my life's work," Curtis says. He refused to get a real job until he discovered green woodworking, and then he didn't have to get one. He's most comfortable making chairs in his shop beyond the garden, but nearly a fourth of his time now is spent teaching chair making. He has published several articles in *Fine Woodworking* magazine and has appeared in other Taunton Press publications.

In 1993, Buchanan, Scott Landis, and Brian Boggs launched a community-based, sustainable forestry project in Honduras called GreenWood. The intent was to make the forest more valuable to its inhabitants, thereby encouraging them to protect their surroundings and their livelihood. The three men taught green wood chair making, using low-tech tools and lesser-known species, much the way that chair making had been pursued in the southern Appalachians. Because of their efforts, at least 30 chair makers, living in the mountainous rainforest along the northern coast, find markets for their production. GreenWood has partnered with the World Wildlife Fund, Mystic Seaport, and The Nature Conservancy to supply lumber certified by the FSC (Forest Stewardship Council) and other products made locally from Honduran hardwoods.

Paradoxically, Curtis seems to live by one of his mottos: "Do nothing. Life's too short to waste time."

Gallery

A commonality among stick chair makers (Windsors, post and rung, and twig) is the challenge of producing a long lasting, round, mortise and tenon joint. Unlike its rectangular cousin, the round mortise, with its large percentage of end grain, makes for a poor glue surface. For centuries chair makers have used other methods, such as super-drying the tenon below measurable moisture content, keeping the mortised stock at equilibrium moisture content, and pounding a slightly oversized tenon (+ $\frac{5}{1000}$ inch) into the mortise. The members of my gallery are some of the finest chair makers working today. They all have refined this joint to fit their styles and needs. Their methods may vary, but the results are the same: a joint that can stand the test of time.

I start with **Dave Sawyer** because, without his selfless help, I would not be a chair maker. Dave's pure pursuit of excellence and his willingness to share are contagious.

John D. Alexander, Jr. is a relentless researcher who no doubt has logged more hours running tests on the round mortise and tenon joint than the next ten chair makers combined. His book, *Make a Chair from a Tree* (Astragal Press, 1994), has influenced chair makers for more than 25 years. When John calls, I pull up a chair and get comfortable for a very detailed discussion.

The summer I met Dave Sawyer he was living on **Drew Langsner**'s farm. A few years later Drew gave me my first opportunity to teach chair making. Drew's school, Country Workshops, which is located in Marshall, North Carolina, has served quality meals and chair making instruction for 30 years.

When David Pye coined the term "craftsmanship of risk" as an alternative to "handmade," he must have been speaking of the way **Tom Lynch** cuts rung tenons for his twig chairs. Lining up the rung by sight with the lathe bed, he moves his whole body forward, pushing the rung into a very large tenon cutter turning at a high rate of speed. It requires a steady hand moving with confidence. One miscue and the lathe gets to use the rung as a weapon against your body. Tom's twig chairs are a wonderful blend of fun and creative freedom.

Of all my many influences, I count that of **Brian Boggs** as the greatest. Through the years, we have bored our wives with thousands of hours of chair talk, over as many beers. Brian's ability to see his work with fresh eyes each day is enviable.

DAVID SAWYER
Balloon-Back Chair, Baluster, 1998

37 x 19 x 20 inches (94 x 48.3 x 50.8 cm)
Basswood, maple, oak, milk paint
PHOTO © JAMIE COPE

DAVID SAWYER
Continuous Arm High Chair, 1987

36 x 20 x 18 inches (91.4 x 50.8 x 45.7 cm)
Butternut, cherry, oak, clear oil finish
PHOTO © JAMIE COPE
COLLECTION OF ANN SAWYER

DAVID SAWYER
Triple Settee, 1996

37 x 70 x 20 inches (94 x 177.8 x 50.8 cm)
Butternut, cherry, oak, clear oil finish
PHOTO © ARTIST

DAVID SAWYER
Sack-Back Rocker-Writer, 1984

42 x 34 x 32 inches (106.7 x 86.4 x 81.3 cm)
Pine, maple, oak, milk paint
PHOTO © JAMIE COPE
COLLECTION OF PAT PRITCHETT

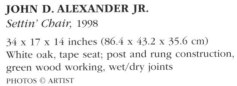

JOHN D. ALEXANDER JR.
Settin' Chair, 1998

34 x 17 x 14 inches (86.4 x 43.2 x 35.6 cm)
White oak, tape seat; post and rung construction,
green wood working, wet/dry joints
PHOTOS © ARTIST

DREW LANGSNER
Hearth Chair #5, 2000

35 x 27 x 26 inches (88.9 x 68.6 x 66 cm)
Red oak, elm seat, oil finish
PHOTO © ARTIST

THOMAS LYNCH

Twig-Back Chair, 2005

46 x 28 x 17 inches
(116.8 x 71.1 x 43.2 cm)
American hornbeam, hickory bark
PHOTO © TOM MCCOLLEY

THOMAS LYNCH

Twig-Back Armchair, 2004

48 x 26 x 18 inches
(121.9 x 66 x 45.7 cm)
American hornbeam, hickory bark
PHOTO © ARTIST

THOMAS LYNCH

Woven-Back Rocker, 2004

48 x 27 x 32 inches
(121.9 x 68.6 x 81.3 cm)
American hornbeam, hickory bark
PHOTO © ARTIST

THOMAS LYNCH

Corner Throne, 2002

38 x 30 x 30 inches (96.5 x 76.2 x 76.2 cm)
American hornbeam, curly maple, hickory bark
PHOTO © TOM MCCOLLEY

THOMAS LYNCH

Rocker, 2005

46 x 24 x 18 inches (116.8 x 61 x 45.7 cm)
Walnut, hickory bark
PHOTO © ARTIST

Curtis Buchanan

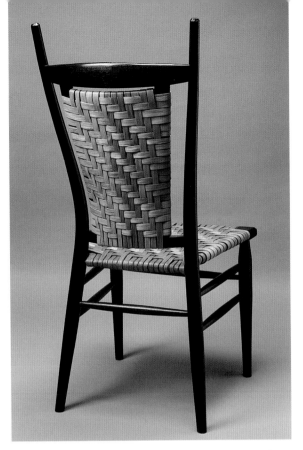

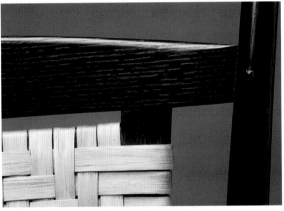

BRIAN BOGGS
Three-Slat Ladder-Back, circa mid-1990s

36 x 19 x 22 inches (91.4 x 48.3 x 55.9 cm)
Cherry, hickory bark; steam bent
PHOTO © GEOF CARR

BRIAN BOGGS
Woven-Back Dining Chair, circa 2002

36 x 19 x 22 inches (91.4 x 48.3 x 55.9 cm)
White oak, hickory bark; steam bent, ebonized
PHOTOS © GEOF CARR

BRIAN BOGGS
Sculpted Fan-Back Rocker, 2003

42 x 28 x 40 inches (106.7 x 71.1 x 101.6 cm)
Walnut, leather; sculpted joinery, steam bent,
ebonized
PHOTO © GEOF CARR

Doug Sigler

Doug Sigler says that he has always designed with function foremost in his mind, but the forms he makes show that beauty and proportion figure strongly in the equation as well. The houses he builds display this attention on a large scale. The division and enlargement of their spaces is carefully thought out so that even a small house belies its compact size with varied and lengthy sight lines. Perhaps his most creative acts, however, have resulted from maintaining close relationships with his students and friends, with whom he collaborates.

DOUG SIGLER
Bench, 2000

36 x 72 x 30 inches (91.4 x 182.9 x 76.2 cm)
Cherry; laminated

Teaching/Learning

My life has been filled with teachers and collaborators. I've been lucky to have had the best of each. I was a student in colleges for 40 years, despite the fact that my guidance counselor said I wouldn't last more than three months there. During a significant amount of that time, I got paid for teaching, while my students and colleagues added to my knowledge.

I did learn a few woodworking basics in my high school industrial arts class, and in my senior year I discovered that I could make some money working with wood in my hometown of Red Hook, New York. I took on a few projects for family, neighbors, and friends, and I knew that I had found my vocation. I was accepted at several state schools as an industrial arts major, but, thanks to my mother's advice, I enrolled at the Rochester Institute of Technology.

The School for American Craftsmen (as it was called then) at R.I.T. had eight instructors, and of the eight, only one was an American, Hobart Cowles, a master of ceramics. In my first year I met Tage Frid, the Danish head of the furniture program, who became my mentor and friend. A man who valued technique and function, Tage's teachings became the foundation of my own work in furniture design and home building. R.I.T. was the only school at the time offering an M.F.A. in furniture design,

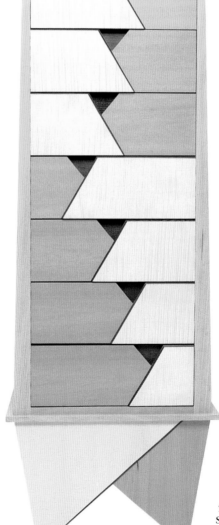

so I stayed on another two years and studied with Wendell Castle and Bill Keyser. Both were my instructors in and out of the classroom. I worked for each of them in their shops during my last years as a student.

Thinking back, I may have been Wendell's first employee. I worked with him building a now-famous music rack and a chest of drawers that were shown in the Museum of Modern Art (see page 106). One day I showed him a sketch of a chair I had designed. He was about to start "stacking" a piece of his own and suggested that my chair might work out well using what he called the "bricklaying" method of stacking. I took his suggestion. The chair, like much of my work, has simple massing and straight lines, while Wendell's work is often more organic and curvilinear. It sits proudly in my home, a reminder of his influence (see page 93).

Bill Keyser demonstrated his impeccable craftsmanship and shared his steam-bending techniques with me while I was a graduate student and sometime employee in his shop. His influence, too, still resonates in my work. In later years I returned to teach in R.I.T.'s wood program

DOUG SIGLER
Victoria Secrets, 1998

58 x 20 x 20 inches (147.3 x 50.8 x 50.8 cm)
Solid pearwood, curly maple, wenge
PHOTO © ARTIST

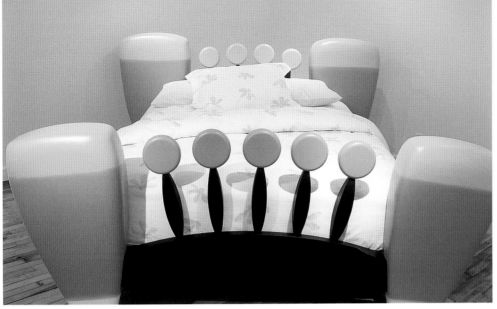

DOUG SIGLER
Trick or Treat, 2000

Queen size
Painted cherry
PHOTO © ARTIST

with Bill. We were opposite personalities in many ways, but we became a team in teaching and developed a friendship that endured 25 years of sharing a tiny office space. You could always tell which desk was his; Bill's showed wide areas of clear wood grain, while mine displayed only the accumulated grains of my life.

I was teaching at Buffalo State College when Bill Brown became the director of Penland School of Crafts. Skip Johnson, Penland's first resident artist and a fellow R.I.T. graduate, suggested that Bill invite me to teach a summer session. The school's workshops offered an alternative learning experience, one in which I immediately felt at home. I returned to Penland year after year.

Bill Brown was dedicated to his students and faculty. He opened his home and all the school's resources to craftspeople willing to try new work. Bill supported them at every turn. He was a talented teacher and sculptor with an open sense of humor. He had an instinctive ability to make each of his invited faculty feel as if they hung the moon. Bill was a stubborn man, too. When he took on a project as grand as the directorship or as common as cleaning a shop space, he held himself and everybody else—staff, faculty, and students alike—hard on the task at hand. Bill taught me a lot about friendship, loyalty, and the need for freedom in the creative process.

DOUG SIGLER
Chopping Block #2

Solid cherry
PHOTO © ARTIST

DOUG SIGLER
Untitled

32 x 32 x 36 inches (81.3 x 81.3 x 91.4 cm)
Solid walnut; stacked, laminated, brick laid

DOUG SIGLER
Orchard Park House, 1982
PHOTO © ARTIST

While teaching at Buffalo State College in the '60s, I opened a craft gallery, Benchmark Studio, with colleague and jeweler Jack Jauquet. I developed a production line including cutting boards, chess sets, bud vases, salt and pepper shakers, and desk accessories that were to be the bread and butter sales. We enjoyed some success but also found out just how demanding production work and gallery ownership could be. It increased my understanding of and respect for both jobs. I've talked often with my students about this experience. I had learned a lot about the flip side of being a production craftsperson. The gallery owner's job is one that deserves respect, too. There's the trust you must gain and keep with the artists and with the public; the challenge of acquiring good work; keeping up with display, sales, overhead—the potential for success and failure. In addition to visiting wood shops and galleries, I exposed my classes to the hectic world of national craft fairs. They developed small production lines, exhibited their work, and tackled the problems involved in producing, pricing, marketing, and selling.

My design philosophy is fairly simple. First and foremost, everything I design has a functional purpose. Because that's a driving force in my work,

you won't find a lot of applied color, or decorative or fantasy elements. I'm definitely not opposed to these treatments; they just don't have priority in my work. Size is also a significant factor for me. For example, I've made a 9-foot round bed, 30-foot conference table, 20-foot, 1800-pound shuffleboard, etc. Working on this scale might have led me to build houses.

My teaching and personal philosophy is also fairly simple: Don't talk about it; do it. Mistakes are an important part of the learning process. When you talk a design idea to death, you don't have the chance to experience the progress of a project. Some of the problems will be solved as you go along; some can be recognized during the sketch phase, while others are better grappled with when you actually work with the materials. By the time you talk yourself into the first piece, you could have made two—one to learn on and a second with refinements taken from what you've learned making the first one.

I began teaching with a three-year commitment in mind, but it didn't take me long to realize that the students had become the major focus of my energy. The students in R.I.T.'s wood program were the best of the best. They gave back as much as I was able to give. I continue to be amazed by the

DOUG SIGLER
Shuffleboard, 1996

28 inches x 24 inches x 21 feet
(71.1 cm x 61 cm x 6.4 m)
Maple, epoxy finish
PHOTO © ARTIST

An example of the signature piece Doug Sigler creates in each house he builds—a private care compartment (toilet paper holder) 8 inches (20.3 cm) in diameter, made from PVC pipe.

A drawing of a barn Doug Sigler reconstructed in 1975
PHOTO © ARTIST

talent, creative thought, enthusiastic conversation, and drive they've brought to my life.

My teaching positions afforded me the opportunity to travel. A three-week workshop in Korea was my most enjoyable and educational trip. I had to use an interpreter, but I soon found that the students and I were able to communicate pretty clearly through drawings and three-dimensional mockups. While I was teaching, the Korean government invited me to extend my stay for another three weeks to work on a design project. The *Sigler Chair* that resulted from our collaboration is, I believe, still being manufactured. I enjoyed the workshop especially, because it demonstrated so clearly that we work in a medium that transcends language. Questions were asked and suggestions offered by graphic means. They seldom required verbal explanation.

My work outside of teaching consisted largely of commissions for furniture and kitchens. I enjoyed working within the parameters set by the clients. The challenge of meeting their objectives while injecting my own style and technique satisfied me. My students were often looking for temporary employment, and they became collaborators on these projects, contributing their ideas and sweat to the process. Some of those students have become colleagues and friends, and the collaborations continue. It's a theme of my life, really. Former students John Dodd, Terry Hunt, Kevin Stark, and Bob Leverich head my speed dial list. We share ideas and

argue about solutions. Arguing is, of course, part of my definition of a successful collaboration.

I've had a residency program of sorts at my home and studio for many years. Former School for American Crafts students have moved into our "bunkhouse" or the guest apartment adjacent to my shop and have stayed for a summer, a year, or longer. They commit one day a week to working for me; in exchange, I provide housing and shop access. Each has enjoyed the bonus of excellent meals now and then, put together by my wife, Kathie. The Sigler Compound has sheltered some fine craftspeople, who have gone on to exceptional careers teaching, creating recognized work in their own studios, or working in the wood/furniture industry. When I had a large project in the works—a furniture commission, kitchen, or house to build—I could offer them full employment for longer periods. All of them were energetic,

DOUG SIGLER
Sigler Chair, 1994

32 x 18 x 24 inches
(81.3 x 45.7 x 61 cm)
Laminated walnut, wenge, aluminum, upholstery
IMAGE COURTESY OF USSO FURNITURE COMPANY, SEOUL, KOREA

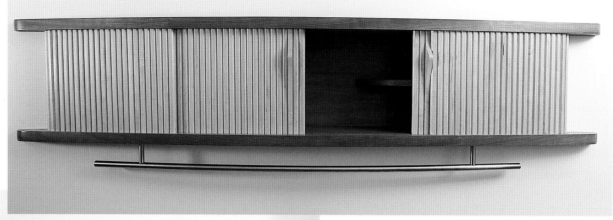

DOUG SIGLER
*Tamboured Medicine Cabinet with
Stainless Steel Towel Bar,* n.d.
14 x 10 x 48 inches (35.6 x 25.4 x 121.9 cm)
Maple, cherry; tambour

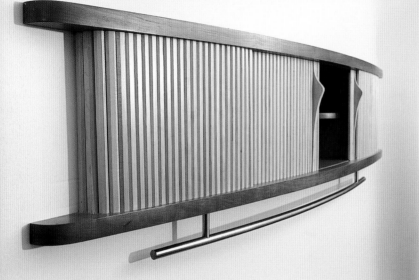

creative, hardworking, and fun-loving—great collaborators once again. They all grew from the experience and furthered the skills and talents they brought with them to these mountains.

Since leaving R.I.T., I've enjoyed the challenges and change of scale involved in building homes. I've collaborated on designs with my friend and former student Bob Leverich. Bob is an accomplished architect as well as a woodworker and sculptor. He sketches concepts, and we work back and forth to develop the plan, the construction strategy, and the details, balancing livability and practicality. We try to include something unexpected or special in each house, such as the bench illustrated on page 91. Sam Reynolds, a student in several of my Penland workshops and a skilled landscape architect, has lent a hand in setting the stage on a number of the house sites, teaching me the importance of carefully considered positioning and approaches for each project.

These collaborations have been both practical and fun. I've set out to build houses and studios that I'd love to live in myself, figuring somebody will feel the same way, buy the house, and make it a home. A cocky attitude, maybe, but it's worked out pretty well. And hey, I'm retired! This is my idea of enjoying life.

The fullness that students and colleagues from Buffalo State, R.I.T., and Penland have brought to my life is amazing, and it's a great feeling for me to see so many of my students exceed my abilities and my imagination in building careers as artists, designers, and craftspeople.

I've passed along the benefits of my experiences, successes, and failures; and my students and colleagues have given back their energy, creativity, divergent viewpoints, and support. We've all collaborated in a continual learning experience.

DOUG SIGLER AND BOB LEVERICH
Patton House, 1997

3700 square feet (1,127.8 square m)
PHOTO © ARTISTS

DOUG SIGLER
Dovetailed Kitchen
Peninsula, 2003

36 x 40 x 96 inches
(91.4 x 101.6 x 243.8 cm)
Cherry

Hands On

Doug Sigler concentrates on building houses, but in each one he finds occasions for his furniture designs. Often these take the form of site-specific vignettes, such as a slim cabinet designed for the restricted sight lines of a bathroom. In the case of this built-in bench, which hovers between an open upstairs hall and the living room below, he had to consider all angles and structural strength as well. Doug shows how he builds an efficient and accurate two-part laminating mold for the bench slats.

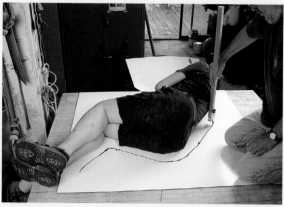

1. Ergonomics can be addressed using charts, graphs, and calculation, but the obvious works better for me, so I trace the body in a comfortable position, using a marker taped to a stick held vertically. I'm looking for a general contour. One-quarter-inch hardboard works well for this template. Because the curves are tight, a two-part mold will be necessary.

2. The ends of the traced line are extended to provide extra room at the ends of the lamination so that it will run out smoothly and to allow for trimming. The line is cut on the band saw to make a template. I try to smooth the traced line as I go, to minimize fairing of the curves.

3. With the template clamped to a piece of ¾-inch AC plywood, a router with a template guide is used to cut a ⅜-inch-wide groove. That should equal the stacked thickness of 16 layers of veneer. So that the bottom of the plywood doesn't tear out, only two-thirds of its thickness is cut with the router.

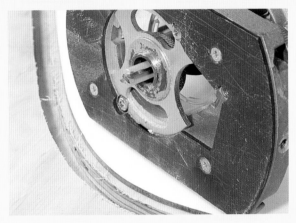

4. The template guide allows for routing a shallow groove, while making the seat contour only slightly larger. The guide must be kept tight against the template for its whole length, because both sides of the groove will form mold faces.

5. I check to make sure that the stack has the right number of veneer layers. The package should fit snugly in the groove.

6. The groove is sawn carefully to split it down its center. There are now two pieces, the first layer of both the top and bottom of the mold.

7. Where the band saw won't fit, a saber saw finishes the cut.

8. With the plywood upside down, a bottom-bearing flush trim bit follows the original slot, thereby trimming the waste from both mold pieces.

Doug Sigler

9. After cutting the second layer of the mold ⅛-inch oversize, this layer gets glued or screwed to the first piece. Then a flush trim bit cuts away the excess.

11. Here's the mold showing the space for 16 layers of veneer. Note the spacer blocks screwed to the bottom to make room for bar clamp heads. Alignment pins are screwed to the mold, both front and back.

12. The 16 layers of veneer are cut in a stack on the band saw, using a one-point rip fence. This is a safer and surer method than ripping the stack on a table saw.

10. The previous step is repeated until the form reaches the desired thickness. To keep the mold flat and straight, each new layer is trimmed to the previous one.

13. Some waxed paper or a plastic sheet and all the gluing supplies have been gathered ready before beginning the glue-up. I use Unibond glue, a liquid with a catalyst. It offers 20 minutes of working time, and it doesn't creep. I mix six parts of liquid and one part of catalyst.

Doug Sigler

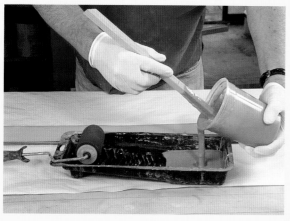

14. The pan makes filling the roller easier, of course, but the larger surface area of the glue also extends its pot life a bit.

15. The glue is rolled evenly on both mating surfaces of veneer.

16. Both sides of the laminate sandwich get release layers of waxed paper.

17. The mold has been waxed for easy release of the cured laminate. The sandwich should be kept close to the bottom curve to minimize shifting along its length. Still, some adjustment is always needed.

18. One layer of veneer was put in the mold previously to mark the length of the laminate. Now we can check for proper alignment on either end.

19. Starting clamping at the deepest point on a curve minimizes strain on the alignment pins.

Doug Sigler

20. Enough clamps are employed to ensure even pressure on the sandwich, indicated by even glue squeeze-out along its whole length.

21. When the glue has cured, one edge of the laminate gets jointed straight.

22. With the jointed edge against the table-saw rip fence, the laminate is trimmed to its finished width. This slat is ready for sanding.

23. I laminate the front and back supports for the bench, instead of cutting them from solid stock, to avoid weakness caused by short grain from cutting curves in solid lumber. The supports are laminated from 12 pieces of cherry in a vacuum press over a male mold. The cherry pieces are each ⅛ inch thick, 4 inches wide, and 8 feet long.

24. I'm using Unibond glue and a waxed mold made similarly to the two-part mold. While the vacuum pump sucks air from the bag, the sandwich ends should be held tight to the mold to prevent the bag from getting between them and ruining the laminate.

25. I've attached the front and back supports to two pieces of plywood representing the walls that the bench will connect. With the slats held in place by double-sided carpet tape and after I've checked for the correct spacing, this simple marking gauge establishes trim lines at the bottoms of the slats.

Doug Sigler

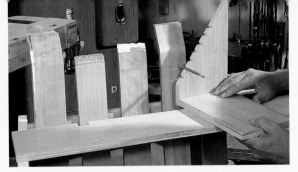

26. I use the same gauge at a different height to mark the slat tops from the back support.

27. For a perfect fit to the installation walls, the arms are scribed with a pencil held flat against the temporary walls. I added a horizontal piece—sawn from solid cherry because it didn't need to add strength—to the back of the back support. That piece matches the wall caps visible in the photo above and continues their line around the bench.

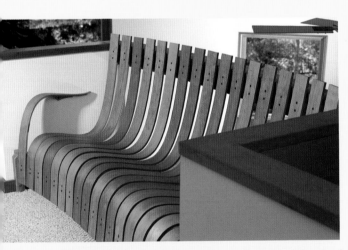

28. All of the bench pieces are sanded and finished separately, and the slats are fastened with carefully positioned decorative screws. The bench hangs on vertical blocks anchored to the walls. The blocks engage slots routed in the ends of the front and back supports. These slots end short of the top edges of the supports. The bench slides down onto the blocks, while small cleats hold the bench arms.

About the Artist

After graduate school at the Rochester Institute of Technology, Doug Sigler began his teaching career at Buffalo State College. He built himself a house in Orchard Park, New York, setting a pattern that he maintained through most of the rest of his life—living in a Sigler house some distance from where he taught. Although he kept a place in Rochester, by the end of the '70s he also lived in Penland, North Carolina. He had taught at Penland and formed a bond with director Bill Brown, which impelled him to buy land nearby. In the summer of 1978, he brought a group of his woodworking students from R.I.T. to help him start building his home there. Thereafter, he divided his time between Rochester and Penland. His wife, Kathie, stayed in Penland—a strong incentive for frequent North Carolina sojourns.

Sigler has built four other homes in the Penland area, most since his retirement. His houses are remarkable for their sense of space and flow, and all contain examples of his built-in cabinetry as well as his signature in-wall toilet paper holder.

He has maintained contact with many of his former students, helping to direct them to better opportunities and suggesting solutions for the design and technical problems they bring to him. As a gesture of their respect, more than 100 former students and colleagues threw a belated surprise retirement party for Doug in October, 2005. Students from 30 years ago and from all over the country traveled to North Carolina to attend.

The only sense in which Doug Sigler has retired is that he no longer receives a paycheck for his teaching. He continues to teach (now in a much larger classroom), to make his own work, and to collaborate in the largest sense of the word.

Gallery

Selecting people and work to be represented in this gallery was not an easy task. There are so many who have my admiration and have influenced my work and life.

I have to begin with professor, mentor, and friend **Tage Frid**. He not only taught me the techniques I have used through the years, but shared the "tricks" and instilled a strong sense of integrity laced with humor. My work has leaned heavily towards function, definitely a trait I picked up from Tage. He preached and practiced with a driving work ethic grounded in the belief that a good craftsman can and should make a living from his craft.

I owe **Bill Brown** personally for making me a part of his family. He took me on as a son; his support was unconditional. Bill often spoke of how important having a strong partner was in his life and career. He valued his wife Jane's accomplishments and credited her with much of his success. I like to think his guidance steered me toward the relationship I enjoy today with my wife, Kathie. I thank Bill for the gifts of time, space, and encouragement he shared with so many craftspeople, encouragement that led to the artist residency program he created at Penland.

While working for **Wendell Castle**, our break-time conversation usually wandered off from the piece we were working on to the next piece, and to the next year, and to what he planned for the next five years and longer. While working with Wendell I discovered it was more important to think ahead, improve, and discover than it was to fall in love with the piece we were currently creating. Looking back, the creative time line Wendell set for himself was very accurate. I've always admired his ability to push the envelope. Wendell continues to bring notoriety to the woodworking world, creating furniture that he has raised to an art form.

John Dodd earned my respect when he was a student, and he has become both a colleague and a friend. I have admired his work from the very beginning. John has a wonderful sense of detail and proportion. His selection of fine veneer and his ability to integrate it with glass, concrete, marble, or any material he may be experimenting with is mind bending. I love his philosophy: simple elegance serves the function.

Early on, I was impressed with designers such as **Mies van der Rohe** and **Marcel Breuer** for the boldness of their designs, their generous scale, and the expansive use of glass to bring light and vistas to their interiors. Breuer's furniture designs were bold and direct in the way he expressed materials and structure.

Bill Keyser shared his experience and enthusiasm. He helped me develop teaching skills that served me well throughout my career. He is an impeccable craftsman who, by example, shows that we are all forever students with much to learn. He retired from R.I.T.'s wood shop to go on and earn a second M.F.A. in painting. Bill strives for excellence, inspiring all of us who have been a part of his life.

Bob Leverich, my Renaissance man, is a licensed architect with a background in ceramics and sculpture, who also earned an M.F.A. in Woodworking and Furniture Design. His drawing ability is the best I've ever seen. He brings all that experience to his teaching in interdisciplinary programs at Evergreen State College in Washington, and to his regular collaborations with me. Bob is one reason I haven't managed to retire—I keep building homes he's designed.

Doug Sigler

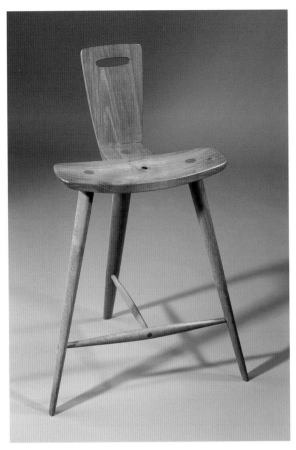

TAGE FRID

3-Legged Stool, early 1960s

22 x 18 x 12 inches
(55.9 x 45.7 x 30.5 cm)
Walnut
BY PERMISSION OF THE ARTIST'S FAMILY

WENDELL CASTLE

Last Chance, 2001

52 x 34 x 34 inches (132.1 x 86.4 x 86.4 cm)
Douglas fir, jelutong, copper
PHOTO © STEVE LABUZETTA

BILL BROWN SR.

Cooperation, 1983

24 x 8 x 11 inches (61 x 20.3 x 27.9 cm)
Welded steel
BY PERMISSION OF THE ARTIST'S FAMILY

WENDELL CASTLE
Chest of Drawers, 1962
47¼ x 52⅜ x 20⁷⁄₁₆ inches
(120 x 64.5 x 51.9 cm)
Oak, walnut, birch, oak plywood

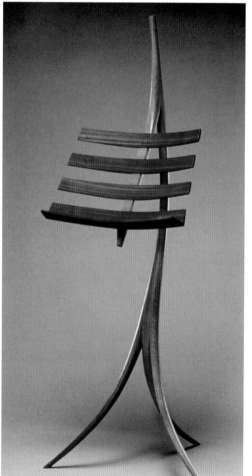

WENDELL CASTLE
Music Stand, 1964

39 x 20 x 16 inches (99.1 x 50.8 x 40.6 cm)
Oak, rosewood; laminated

JOHN DODD
Foyer Mirror, 1994

80 x 21 x 17 inches (203.2 x 53.3 x 43.2 cm)
Ebonized cherry, Douglas fir beam, mirror
PHOTO © WOODY PACKARD

JOHN DODD
Foyer Bench, 1994

18 x 68 x 24 inches (45.7 x 172.7 x 61 cm)
Douglas fir beams, ebonized cherry;
cantilevered
PHOTO © WOODY PACKARD

JOHN DODD
Vertigo, 2002

90 x 19 x 17 inches (228.6 x 48.3 x 43.2 cm)
Mahogany, lacewood, copper lamp shade,
ebony and steel details, holly interiors; curved
PHOTOS © WOODY PACKARD

JOHN DODD
Wall Niche, 1995

80 x 13 x 12 inches (203.2 x 33 x 30.5 cm)
Makore, mahogany, granite, mirror; laminated
PHOTO © WOODY PACKARD

LUDWIG MIES VAN DER ROHE
Farnsworth House, Plano, Illinois, 1951

1700 square feet (157.9 square m)
PHOTO © JON MILLER, HEDRICH BLESSING
COURTESY OF LANDMARKS PRESERVATION COUNCIL OF ILLINOIS

MARCEL BREUER
Wassily Chair, 1925

28¼ x 31 x 27½ inches (71.8 x 78.7 x 69.9 cm)
Seamless tubular steel with chromed finish, cowhide
PHOTO COURTESY OF KNOLL, INC.

WILLIAM A. KEYSER JR.

Cross, 1997

72 x 30 x 5 inches (182.9 x 76.2 x 12.7 cm)
Walnut, oil finish; laminated, shaped
PHOTO © DAVID J. LEVEILLE
COURTESY OF NAZARETH COLLEGE INTERFAITH CHAPEL,
PITTSFORD, NY

WILLIAM A. KEYSER JR.

Altar, 1997

39 x 40 x 40 inches (99.1 x 101.6 x 101.6 cm)
White oak, catalyzed lacquer; mortise and
tenon joinery, veneered
PHOTOS © DAVID J. LEVEILLE
COURTESY OF ST. PIUS TENTH CHURCH, CHILI, NY

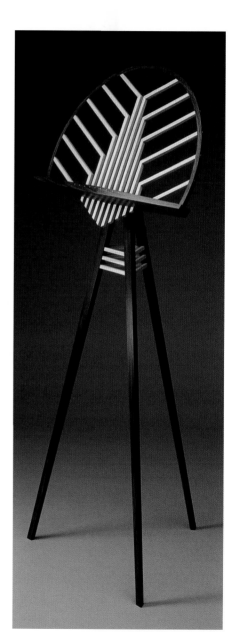

WILLIAM A. KEYSER JR.

Music Stand, 1990

49 x 24 x 24 inches (124.5 x 61 x 61 cm)
Rosewood, ash, oil finish; laminated
PHOTO © DAVID J. LEVEILLE
PRIVATE COLLECTION

Doug Sigler

WILLIAM A. KEYSER JR.
Subway Bench, 1984

48 x 84 x 360 inches
(121.9 x 213.4 x 914.4 cm)
Maple, stainless steel, epoxy, spar
varnish; stack lamination
PHOTO © BOB ANDRUSZKIEWICZ
COURTESY OF ALEWIFE STATION,
MASSACHUSETTS BAY TRANSPORTATION
AUTHORITY, CAMBRIDGE, MA

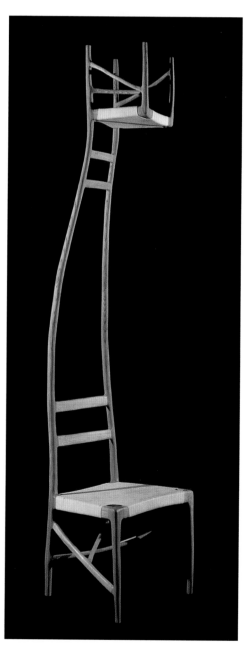

R.T. LEVERICH
Crib, 1992

17 x 24 x 21 inches (43.2 x 61 x 53.3 cm)
Red cedar
PHOTO © EARL KAGE MUSEOGRAPHICS
PRIVATE COLLECTION

R.T. LEVERICH
Father/Son Chair, 1989

85 x 18 x 17 inches (215.9 x 45.7 x 43.2 cm)
Ash, rawhide
PHOTO © EARL KAGE MUSEOGRAPHICS
PRIVATE COLLECTION

Brent Skidmore

Brent Skidmore's sculpture and sculptural furniture display his quest for repose through careful composition of disparate forms. The pieces have considerable visual motion while remaining unified. In addition to form and color, Skidmore uses positive and negative textures to enliven his work. In demonstrating one of his texturing methods, he shows how the "Ming Ding" process lends itself to variety and innovation.

BRENT SKIDMORE
Low Slung Boulders, 2005

54 x 24 x 17 inches (137.2 x 61 x 43.2 cm)
Ash, basswood, glass, acrylic paints

Form Follows Dysfunction

With a B.F.A. and an M.F.A. in sculpture, an early training in '70s hair design/fashion (Mom), plumbing/hard work (Dad), and the driving impulses of a toddler (greed and curiosity), I have gained at 40 the audacity to call myself an artist. I come from a very humble but supportive background, but I've gone without artistic suffering. I have never been interested in the starving part of being an artist.

My story as an artist began quite early and can be traced to many memories of Etch-A-Sketch in the '60s, black crayon-resist drawings in the '70s, and batiks in the '80s. Most of this work was in two dimensions and largely based on drawing, either observational or imagined. This background, along with my most influential mentor, Millie Fraley, would later lead me to pursue an undergraduate degree in graphic design. Millie taught art at North Bullitt High School, and her encouragement of my endeavors extended to moving out of her office and lending it to me as my private studio.

At Murray State University, I met two other invaluable mentors, Paul Sasso and Steve Bishop. In Steve's 3-D design class, I realized my attraction to

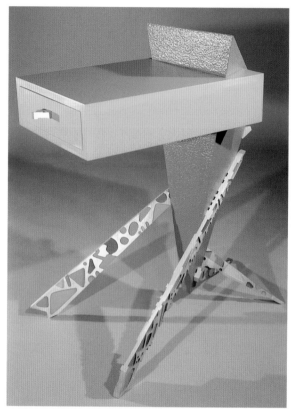

BRENT SKIDMORE
L'Orangatable, 1987

37 x 26 x 24 inches (94 x 66 x 61 cm)
Poplar, cast aluminum, ColorCore
Formica, paint
PHOTO © ARTIST
PRIVATE COLLECTION

BRENT SKIDMORE
Cartage=Internal, 1990
100 x 34 x 48 inches (254 x 86.4 x 121.9 cm)
Poplar, cracked corn, cotton duck, wheels
PHOTO © ARTIST
PRIVATE COLLECTION

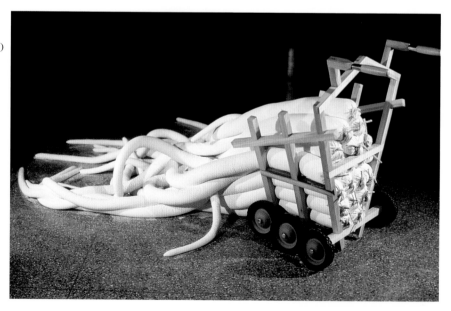

texture, materials, and three-dimensional form. I became hooked on sculpture and the laborious nature of process—the work! I remember the effect my first sand casting in molten aluminum had on me. There it was, the result of my scratching in the mold face: no masterpiece, just texture, texture, texture. I was changed, so I changed my major from graphic design to sculpture that very week.

I immersed myself in the processes of wax, ceramic shell, and molten metal. Paul Sasso visited the sculpture studio frequently and predicted that I'd soon tire of the rigors of metal casting and try wood, a sweeter, gentler material that even smells good. Paul offered me many lessons in materials and technique and never tired of offering encouraging words. I remained focused in the sculpture studio and began to make all pieces of both wood and metal. Steve and Paul, along with our wonderful studios, gave me the exact environment that I needed in order to succeed. I had become a sculptor: someone driven by form, space, color, and texture.

My work in graduate school at Indiana University was that of a mixed media sculptor working primarily with wood, fabrics, and rubber. I was reminded in critique that all my work had some origin in functional objects—whether it was an ironing board, gun, shopping cart, bomb, or farm implements—and that they all looked somewhat like furniture. The human aspect presented itself mostly through a series of works about the coal-mining industry, in which many personal stories were used as inspiration to make functional sculptures.

In 1998 I decided to leave teaching for what I thought would be one year, but which turned into six. During that time I realized the freedom and celebration that comes from making one's living as a working artist. Due mostly to an unfulfilled dream and the stress of self-employment that no one sees until one is in its midst, I have returned to one of my first loves, teaching. During my separation from academia, I had to come to grips with the one aspect of art making no one wants to talk about during college and graduate school: If you are successful at making art, art becomes your job. People forget this. I spent many bittersweet days celebrating my newfound success, while I made the same buffet over again.

I have been fortunate enough to have frequent orders for functional pieces, while maintaining a steady stream of speculative and sometimes much less useful work. A turning point came on the day

BRENT SKIDMORE
"B" Buffet, 2003

37 x 60 x 19 inches (94 x 152.4 x 48.3 cm)
Mahogany, pommelle sapele, wenge, fiddleback maple, birch, acrylic paints
PHOTO © DAVID RAMSEY
PRIVATE COLLECTION

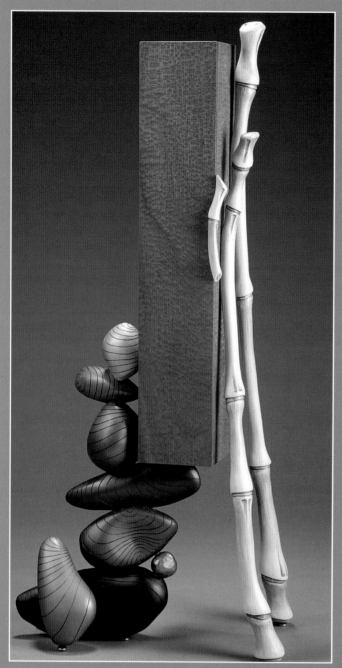

BRENT SKIDMORE
Boo, Pomm, and Boulder, 2003

67 x 32 x 17 inches
(170.2 x 81.3 x 43.2 cm)
Pommele sapele, poplar, basswood, sycamore,
acrylic paints
PHOTO © DAVID RAMSEY
PRIVATE COLLECTION

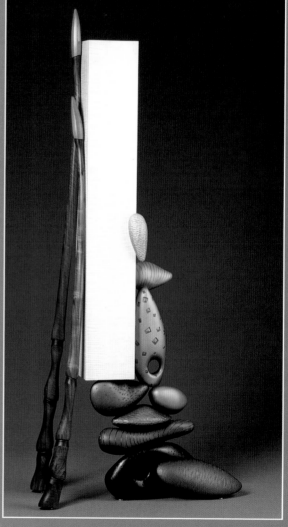

BRENT SKIDMORE
Blonde Variables of a Canyon, 2003

77 x 34 x 16 inches (195.6 x 86.4 x 40.6 cm)
Fiddleback English maple, walnut, basswood, maple,
acrylic paints
PHOTO © DAVID RAMSEY

my good friend Kurt Nielsen said, "You know, Brent, what you need is a box with four legs." On seeing my frustration at repeating many pieces with limited right angles, Kurt suggested making some pieces that were obviously furniture. His remark was a gift, and he in turn has eaten very well at our table since that day. These "boxes with four legs" are very rewarding to make, because they afford me a chance to interact with the client, a person who will actually use the furniture. This really resonates with a guy who for so long made furniture while calling it sculpture and remained unmindful of the power of the long history of furniture.

This connection with the viewer through furniture is important to me, and it fosters visual communication in several ways. Keeping in mind the person who will use and enjoy the piece helps me clarify the often very personal experiences that motivate my art and from which its meaning derives. Then too, working in human scale tends to make the communication more personal and less idiosyncratic. The scale becomes as important as the form, color, or texture and helps beckon us to the meaning of the piece. Furthermore, the fact that furniture must be in some sense functional gives the viewer a comfortable place to begin thinking about what else it is. These factors make me feel I have more power to communicate because of the almost immediate interaction with the viewer/user that they encourage. People simply come closer, both physically and emotionally, and the formal relationships and concepts seem to be conveyed more effectively through furniture.

I design pieces of furniture in which I am always trying to push and question the relationships between furniture history, sculpture, and functional art while expressing myself in as sculptural a way as possible. Constantly striving for a unified whole made up of very different forms, I find that I'm most comfortable making compositions with varied proportions, dissonance, imbalance, and complex formal relationships. The fact that they're furniture helps make them more visually available to interpretation.

BRENT SKIDMORE
Maxwell's Mellow Mirror, 2005
80 x 26 x 15 inches (203.2 x 66 x 38.1 cm)
Basswood, mirror, acrylic paints

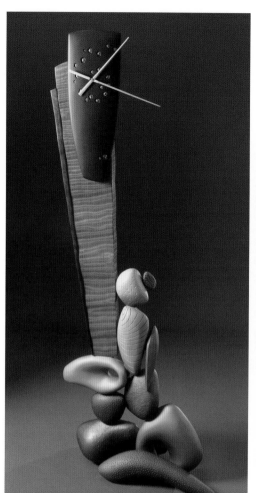

BRENT SKIDMORE
Stuart's Night Time Canyon Sky, 2005
72 x 28 x 15 inches (182.9 x 71.1 x 38.1 cm)
Fiddleback redwood, basswood, walnut, MDF, acrylic paint

Many of my pieces, such as *Stuart's Night Time Canyon Sky* and *Beginning of Balanced Horizon,* look as though they might topple over. Both pieces derive from dreams of my children's future or from current notions of being a father. They are presented in flux to convey the mutable quality of each moment. Living with my two sons, Stuart and Maxwell, makes me reevaluate daily the dynamic balance of life. They are constantly asking me to be here now, and we all know this is a huge task. It may seem that I have many things about my own studio work figured out. On the contrary, I feel as if I am just like Stuart and Maxwell—still learning a language. It's a language I have to practice, over and over, each day, and I have only mastered a few words of it, words like "bliss," "longing," and "imagination."

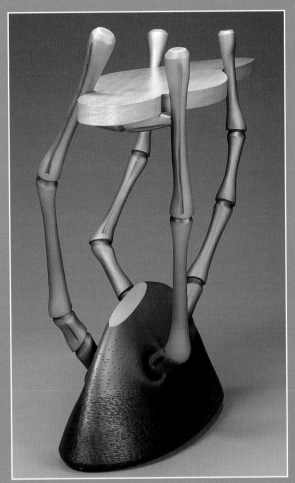

BRENT SKIDMORE
Top Down Boo, 2003

34 x 57 x 18 inches (86.4 x 144.8 x 45.7 cm)
Planetree, poplar, steel, acrylic paints
PHOTO © DAVID RAMSEY
PRIVATE COLLECTION

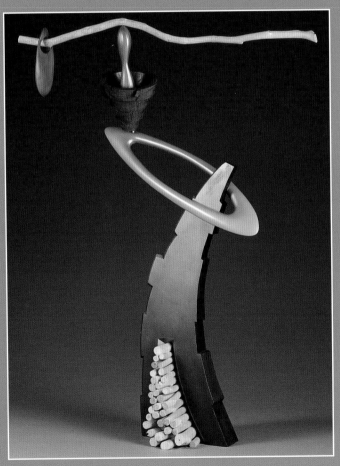

BRENT SKIDMORE
Beginning of Balanced Horizon, 2002

72 x 52 x 20 inches (182.9 x 132.1 x 50.8 cm)
Basswood, poplar, cherry, mountain laurel, aluminum, steel
PHOTO © DAVID RAMSEY
COLLECTION OF RICK AND DANA DAVIS

Hands On

In Brent Skidmore's sculptural furniture, forms hover between rocks or bone fossils and organic entities. Similarly, the variety of those forms might seem to drive them apart, but they find an uneasy repose in the composition itself. The textures he applies beckon the viewer to touch the objects with his eyes. Brent demonstrates his version of an ancient technique to produce a positive texture now dubbed "Ming Ding."

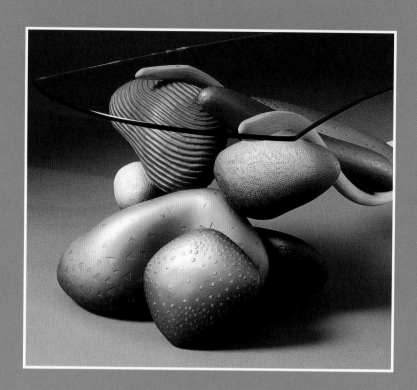

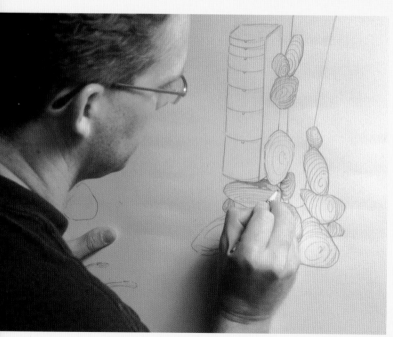

1. I start every piece at my drawing board, a 4-foot-wide roll of white paper connected to a slanted, wall-mounted board. I feel it is important for me to draw standing or perched on a stool to keep me loose and active.

2. Because I begin the carving with a "Lancelot" or "Arbortech" attachment, I use considerable caution and plenty of safety equipment. This includes eye and hearing protection, anti-vibration gloves, a face shield, a leather apron, and a dust mask.

3. From drawings, a full-scale pattern is developed of the front view of the stack of boulder/stone forms and cut out of lauan plywood on this 1950s 14-inch Rockwell saw fitted with an improved Carter bearing set.

4. I use the grinder for many aspects of my carving, but here the roughing-out begins with an aggressive chainsaw cutter head. The guard is missing so that I can get much closer to the work. It's very important to keep both hands on the grinder at all times. The depth of cut is controlled by leaning on the front of the gearbox.

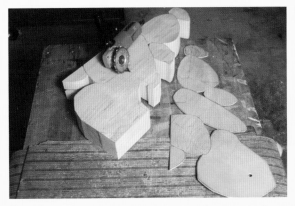

5. After I've established a pattern and dealt with full-scale composition issues through cardboard mock-ups and the patterns, the basswood is dressed, the joinery laid out, a sufficient thickness of stock is glued up, and the silhouette is cut out.

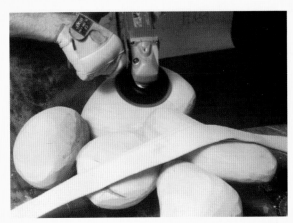

6. An abrasive wheel (of 36 grit) removes the chainsaw marks and further shapes the forms. This is dusty but enjoyable work.

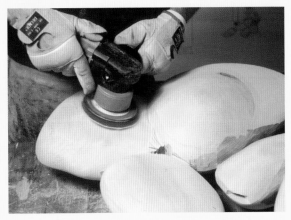

7. The forms are refined and smoothed with a random orbit sander equipped with a contour pad. I use self-adhering pads because the Velcro ones tend to be less flexible.

Brent Skidmore

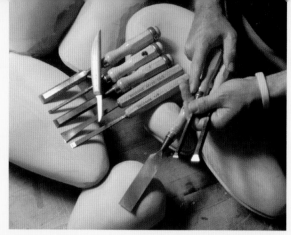

8. The hand carving comes next, using a limited number of carving chisels and a multitude of cabinetmaker's chisels, a couple of knives, and skew chisels. You can do a lot of carving on convex forms by just flipping a straight bench chisel over to use it with the bevel down.

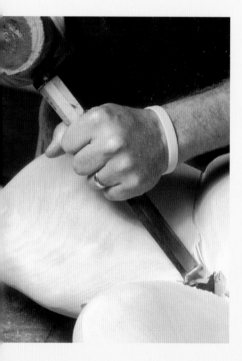

9. Defining the junctions is rewarding quiet work in contrast to all the grinding.

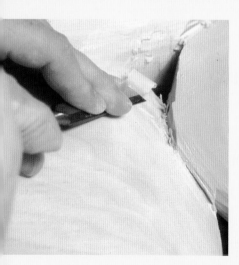

10. This is when I can really start to understand and define the relationships between these forms.

11. Rasps help create more roundness. The Nicholson #49 and #50 pattern maker's rasps are most useful.

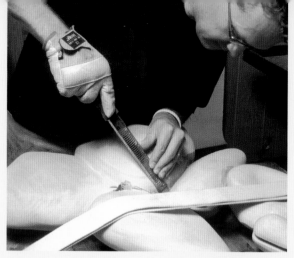

12. All the interior areas are sanded by hand. There's no other way.

13. Once the forms are smooth, the texturing process begins. One of the first surface techniques I used was a simple fluted line to denote the topographical nature of the forms. I have done complete stacks with this simple texture, and I feel the power of the line is unmatched for revealing forms and indicating direction.

14. Another great texture producer and an excellent stress reducer is the sidewalk approach. The older the sidewalk the better—granulation is the key.

15. Most of the tools pictured consist of simple hardware welded to steel handles. Any of these can be used to make negative texture, but those indentations also form the first step in creating a Ming Ding texture. Will Neptune showed me this technique in 1998, and it probably dates from the Ming Dynasty.

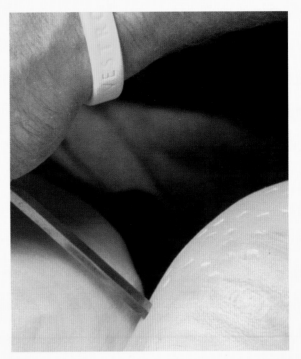

16. To create a true Ming Ding texture, where there is a positive bump, discreet areas of the wood must first be compressed. The tool shown above is a piece of square stock used to make tiny squares. The face is ground flat across, leaving sharp edges that shear the fibers.

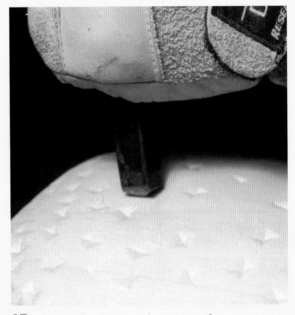

17. Shown above is another piece of square stock, ground with a four-sided point to create a pyramid indentation. I sometimes leave this as an impression because it's hard to control while raising the grain.

Brent Skidmore

18. Here is another favorite. The tool consists of a large washer welded to a steel handle. Striking it twice creates an "X."

19. For the second step in the Ming Ding process, the indented areas are sanded enough to remove bent fibers near the surface and to smooth the area around the dent, but as much as possible of the compressed wood is retained.

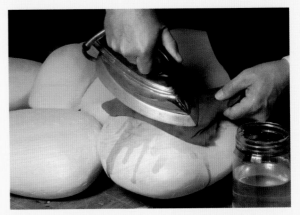

20. The third and final step to getting a great raised texture involves heat and moisture. An iron with a wet cloth expands the compressed fibers until the pattern rises above the surrounding surface. This is basswood; other woods will yield different results and may not expand enough.

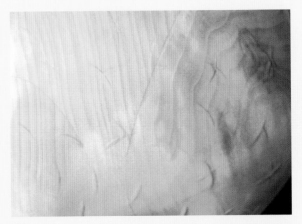

21. Here are the crescents...

22. ...and the small squares raised.

23. Additional forms are added to create more depth. One-half-inch dowels will hold this small form, but steel threaded rods bedded in epoxy offer more strength when joining structural assemblies.

24. The piece is ready for finishing. A glass top completes the coffee table.

About the Artist

In 2004 Brent Skidmore relocated his family to Grand Rapids, Michigan, to take a position at Kendall College of Art and Design of Ferris State University, where he teaches 3-D design and woodworking and functional art, and is a vital part of the college's newly established B.F.A. degree in sculpture and functional art. He maintains his own studio, which he opened in 1998. Before moving to Michigan, he taught for seven years at Central Piedmont Community College in Charlotte, North Carolina. After earning a B.F.A. in Sculpture (1987) at Murray State University, Kentucky, Skidmore received his M.F.A. in Sculpture from Indiana University (1990).

Over the past 15 years Brent has taught many workshops at venues such as Penland School. He has exhibited in more than 100 shows nationally and internationally, including the Smithsonian Craft Show, TAIDE-KA SITYO-TAIDE (Art & Craft from North Carolina) at the Craft Museum of Finland in Jycaskyla, and most recently at SOFA Chicago with Function+Art gallery.

Brent has won several grants and prizes, including the Juror's Award in Furniture at Craftforms 2004, Wayne Art Center, Wayne, Pennsylvania, and two "Emma-grants" to attend the Emma Lake Conference on Collaboration sponsored by the Saskatchewan Craft Council in Saskatoon.

Brent and his dog Patches, 1969
PHOTO © JANICE ROBBINS

Gallery

I am blessed to be able to count all of the people represented here as friends, except for the two who are deceased. What unifies these artists is the desire to create and communicate through well-crafted objects, whether by taking a fresh look at a period piece or making a chair like no other. Paul Sasso and Kurt Nielsen are not represented here because they have chapters in this book, but they remain two of the most important artists who have touched my life and work. I thank Kurt for his constant pursuit of excellence, Paul for his constant encouragement, and both for works that sing of life's intensity, of humor, and of love.

Michael Thonet and **Carlo Mollino** are represented by two of my very favorite pieces. I have always looked to Thonet for his complete understanding of line in furniture and his belief in the techniques he developed for bending and laminating wood. Mollino was a rebel whose brilliance in areas such as avionics, interior design, photography, and architecture has always inspired me.

Clifton Monteith's work leaves me short of words and breath. His pieces are passion translated into a dance of line that the eye cannot resist.

Metalsmith **Barbara Bayne** makes elemental organic forms distinguished by their carefully wrought textures. Barbara's pieces draw you in through their simple intimacy and rich textures.

Dean Pulver makes chairs that are fascinating because they appear to be contemporary versions of nonexistent African chairs. They have elegant, simple forms and bear the rich texture of their maker's hand.

Barbara Holmes's work resonates for me because of its wonderful mixture of furniture forms, science, and the human body. Her pieces provoke questions of scale, use, culture, and meaning.

Canadian **Michael Hosaluk**'s work reveals his zest for life through the use of brilliant color and sexy form. Both Michael and Jamie Russell have impressed upon me the importance of collaboration and therefore the need to heed the work of our predecessors.

Will Neptune's work is that of a consummate craftsman. His period pieces inspire me with their power, a quality many overlook because of their traditional forms. I first met Will in 1998, and he introduced me to the technique depicted in my Hands On section.

In **Jamie Russell**'s work, we see a true understanding of and love for the creatures of the earth. His subtractive approach is inspiring because it leaves no room for error.

Another exemplar in probing questions of culture and form is **Brad Reed Nelson**. His work offers a fresh mix of pop culture, Asian architecture, and striking, powerful forms.

CARLO MOLLINO
Arabesco, 1949

17¹¹⁄₁₆ x 50¹³⁄₁₆ x 20⅞ inches
(44.9 x 129.1 x 53 cm)
Bent plywood, beech, cherry,
stainless steel discs, tempered
glass, varnish; veneered
PHOTO © MARINO RAMAZZOTTI
COURTESY OF THE MANUFACTURER,
ZANOTTA S.P.A., ITALY

MICHAEL THONET
Chair 214, 1859

33 x 17 x 20½ inches (84 x 43 x 52 cm)
Bentwood , woven cane
PHOTO © MICHAEL GERLACH, FRANKFURT, GERMANY
COURTESY OF GEBRÜDER THONET GMBH

CLIFTON MONTEITH
Tall Chair, 2003
54 x 26 x 28 inches (137.2 x 66 x 71.1 cm)
Willow, aspen wood
PHOTOS © JOHN WILLIAMS

BARBARA BAYNE
Two Pierced Beaded Necklaces, 2003

Beads, ¾ x ¾ x ½ inches (1.9 x 1.9 x 1.3 cm);
cable, 16 inches (40.6 cm)
18-karat gold, sterling silver, fine silver; textured,
die formed, pierced, fabricated, oxidized
PHOTO © PAM PERUGI MARRICCINI

BARBARA BAYNE
Pebble Bracelet, 1997

1 x 7¼ x ⅜ inches (2.5 x 18.4 x 1 cm)
Sterling silver; textured, die formed, fabricated
PHOTO © PAM PERUGI MARRICCINI

BARBARA BAYNE
Ten Element Collage Pin/Pendant, 2003

2⅛ x 2¾ x ¼ inches (5.4 x 7 x 0.6 cm)
14-karat gold, silver, fine silver; textured,
die formed, fabricated, oxidized
PHOTO © PAM PERUGI MARRICCINI

DEAN PULVER

Fauna, 2004

35 x 17 x 20 inches (88.9 x 43.2 x 50.8 cm)
Walnut, paint, dye; carved
PHOTO © PAT POLLARD

DEAN PULVER

My Friend's Friend, 2003

28 x 26 x 20 inches (71.1 x 66 x 50.8 cm)
Walnut, dye
PHOTO © PAT POLLARD

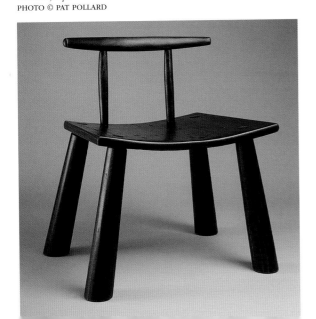

DEAN PULVER

Tall Mirrored Cabinet, 2003

80 x 20 x 10 inches (203.2 x 50.8 x 25.4 cm)
Walnut, padauk, dye; carved
PHOTO © PAT POLLARD

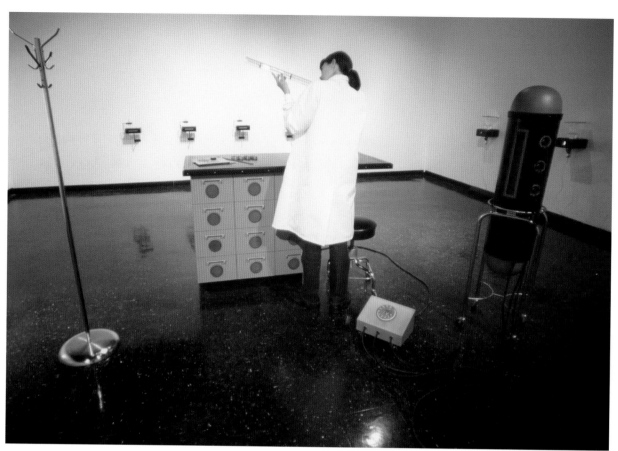

BARBARA HOLMES
The Problem of Logic, 2001

Installation
PHOTO © ARTIST

BARBARA HOLMES
A Solution for Contention, 1999

59 x 28½ x 13 inches (149.9 x 72.4 x 33 cm)
Painted wood, stainless steel, mirror, soap, cotton washcloths
PHOTO © ARTIST
COLLECTION OF JIM CAVOLT

Brent Skidmore

MICHAEL HOSALUK

Untitled, 2005

16 x 20 x 6 inches (40.6 x 50.8 x 15.2 cm)
Arbutus burl; turned, carved, textured
PHOTOS © GRANT KERNAN, AK PHOTO

MICHAEL HOSALUK

Crow, 2004

24 x 28 x 20 inches (61 x 71.1 x 50.8 cm)
Maple, birch, steel, paint
PHOTO © GRANT KERNAN, AK PHOTO

Brent Skidmore

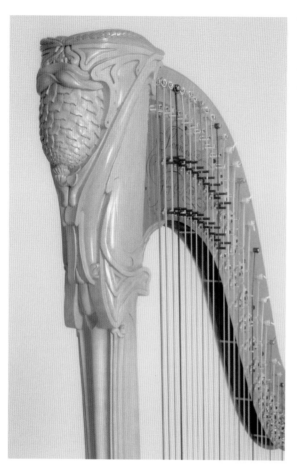

WILL NEPTUNE
Concert Pedal Harp, Art Nouveau Style, detail, 2003

73 x 46 x 18 inches (185.4 x 116.8 x 45.7 cm)
Maple, brass, steel, shellac; carved, laminated
PHOTO © DAVID SITRON, SITRON STUDIOS
COURTESY OF SWANSON HARP COMPANY, EAST BOSTON, MA

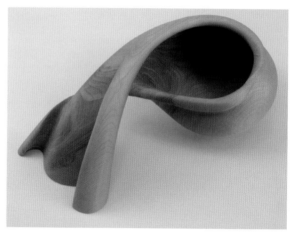

JAMIE RUSSELL
Young Woman Grounded, 2004

4½ x 8 x 5 inches (11.4 x 20.3 x 12.7 cm)
Birch, oil finish; hand carved, machine carved
PHOTO © TRENT WATTS

JAMIE RUSSELL
Sadie the Bitch from Hell, 2001

29 x 54 x 16 inches
(73.7 x 137.2 x 40.6 cm)
Big leaf maple, cherry, glass, oil finish;
turned, hand carved, machine carved
PHOTO © KEVIN HOGARTH
COURTESY OF LEWIS WEXLER GALLERY,
PHILADELPHIA, PA

Brent Skidmore

BRAD REED NELSON

Buildings as Benches, 2005

17 x 15 x 64 inches (43.2 x 38.1 x 162.6 cm)
Reclaimed fir, mahogany, varnish; ebonized, Japanese
lap-joint construction
PHOTO © ARTIST

BRAD REED NELSON

Little Japanese Girl, 2005

16 x 10 x 10 inches (40.6 x 25.4 x 25.4 cm)
Reclaimed fir, mahogany, poplar, ceramic vase, varnish;
ebonized, Japanese lap-joint construction
PHOTO © JENNIFER OUTWATER
CERAMIC VASE COURTESY OF ALLEGHANY MEADOWS

BRAD REED NELSON

Big Mama Little Baby, 2005

Mama, 16 x 9 x 9 inches (40.6 x 22.9 x 22.9 cm);
baby, 10 x 6 x 6 inches (25.4 x 15.2 x 15.2 cm)
Poplar, pear wood, powder-coated steel; turned, sprayed
with auto lacquer, machined
PHOTO © ARTIST

Brent Skidmore

Jere Osgood

 *Like many furniture makers, Jere Osgood has had to invent tools and methods in order to build his designs. Because his furniture derives from organic sources, it is characterized by curved and flowing forms. The lamination technique he pioneered produces strong, curved tapers that appear to have come that way from the tree. In his Hands On section, he demonstrates the process he uses to produce his trademark form, the tapered laminate leg. Jere's work reminds us that technique is only useful when it enables, and is subsumed by, the designed form.*

JERE OSGOOD
Spring Desk, 2005

30 x 27 x 54 inches (76.2 x 68.6 x 137.2 cm)
Claro walnut, ash
PHOTO © DEAN POWELL
COLLECTION OF ARTIST

Design First, Invent Later

There wasn't a beginning to my interest in woodworking. I just grew up with it. All the members of my family had workshops, so when I was small I just made things, and this seemed very natural. On weekends I would help my father put on a roof, install some plumbing, or even hang wallpaper, which I don't expect ever to do again. My father and I also repaired furniture for other members of the family. I didn't realize it at the time, but it was an important learning period. Why did this chair break? What was the best finish for a table?

As I became more skilled at fixing things—say from the age of 10 on—neighbors asked me to repair their furniture. I remember fixing the top of a huge Honduran rosewood dining table. And I remember being fascinated by the joinery in some Chinese tables. It was a version of the sliding dovetail that I still use.

I don't remember much talk of art or artists. There was a poet on my mother's side of the family, and my mother had a good friend from New Zealand who was a painter. These were just natural day-to-day things, but there wasn't any talk about design. I think it took me years to grasp the fact that I was to "design things."

We lived on Staten Island, and sometimes my mother and I would take the ferry to Manhattan, with the Statue of Liberty to our left and the impressive buildings straight ahead. The skyscrapers were so big and the crush of the crowds so alarming, but

JERE OSGOOD
Maple Chair, 1995

35 x 21 x 18 inches (88.9 x 53.3 x 45.7 cm)
Curly maple
PHOTO © DEAN POWELL
PRIVATE COLLECTION

JERE OSGOOD
Wave Table, 1999

28 x 28 x 62 inches (71.1 x 71.1 x 157.5 cm)
Sycamore
PHOTO © DEAN POWELL
COLLECTION OF NEW HAMPSHIRE HISTORICAL SOCIETY, CONCORD, NH

my mother would take me to the Metropolitan Museum of Art as a treat. And I liked that.

If my mother and aunt encouraged me and fed my interest in art, my father and grandfather tended to my more physical side. My father carried on the family ethic: If you want something, make it. For instance, he made his own circular saw, which we used for years. I have just continued that tradition, although for me it comes out more like this: If you want to see something new, you have to make it.

My grandfather was an architect, though he wasn't practicing when I knew him. He specialized in stonework. He would tell me to check out certain details at Grand Central Station in New York or at Union Station in Washington, D.C. I can still remember his workshop with its thousands of pieces of wood and the wonderful smell. He made smaller things like boxes and many bowls on his lathe. I remember his excitement when he found a new piece of wood for a bowl.

Because of my grandfather, I went off to architecture school for a while. Being there meant that I had to learn to draw and design. Up to that point design had not been in my vocabulary. Architecture school taught me how to approach designing: the use of many sketches to search for a form, then making flow diagrams, renderings, and presentations. I was able to carry these methods over to the School for American Craftsmen, at Rochester Institute of Technology, when I went there to study furniture making. Still, the ability to initiate one's own designs comes on slowly. My epiphany came when I saw Wharton Esherick's work. It gave me de facto permission to do what I wanted.

My years at the School for American Craftsmen were really a wonderful time in my life. I got the technical training that I badly needed and was very productive. I don't feel my work was overly original, but I was on the way—building a vocabulary of pieces and developing a three-dimensional mind. In other words, if you design it this way, then this is what it will look like in the final result.

The other strong influence at that time was the year I spent in Denmark. Daniel Jackson, a good friend in school, had gone there to study through an organization called the Scandinavian Seminar. He convinced me to join him for a year after my graduation, before I started work in earnest. Dan

JERE OSGOOD
Spring 90 Desk, 1990
49 x 69 x 41 inches (124.5 x 175.3 x 104.1 cm)
Maccassar ebony, ash
PHOTOS © DEAN POWELL
COLLECTION OF THE MINT MUSEUM OF CRAFT + DESIGN, CHARLOTTE, NC

JERE OSGOOD
Sideboard, 2002

39 x 17 x 49 inches
(99.1 x 43.2 x 124.5 cm)
Walnut, hornbeam
PHOTO © DEAN POWELL
PRIVATE COLLECTION

JERE OSGOOD
Dining Table, 2001

45 x 45 x 29 inches (114.3 x 114.3 x 73.7 cm)
Claro walnut, hornbeam
PHOTO © DEAN POWELL
PRIVATE COLLECTION

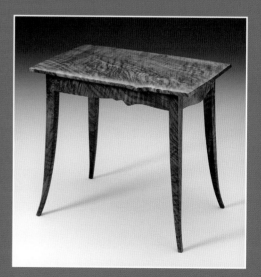

JERE OSGOOD
Owassa Table, 1994

18½ x 14½ x 22 inches (47 x 36.8 x 55.9 cm)
Claro walnut
PHOTO © DEAN POWELL
PRIVATE COLLECTION

JERE OSGOOD
Spring Desk, 1996

49 x 31½ x 51 inches (124.5 x 80 x 129.5 cm)
Bubinga, wenge
PHOTOS © DEAN POWELL
COLLECTION OF CURRIER MUSEUM OF ART, MANCHESTER, NH

introduced me to Peder Moos, and if I had any doubts about my chosen career direction, they were certainly resolved. Peder Moos was the only Danish craftsman who both designed and made his own furniture. He was a very intense person—very involved in his work. The way he approached designing and making made a huge impression on me. It was a good year for me. That was more than 40 years ago, but it's had a long-term effect. I can still speak a little Danish.

When I entered the School for American Craftsmen, I felt there was nothing much new under the sun. Designing was just to be a rearrangement of existing forms. The year in Denmark gave me a chance to think about my years of schooling. I was in the process of breaking through to a new way of working and a more creative way of thinking. My breakthrough, facilitated by the example of Peder Moos and by long talks with Dan Jackson, was to finally see that I could draw on my own personal thoughts about how a piece of furniture should be made and how I needed it to look.

For me furniture is about three-dimensional form. I am concerned with how it functions, how we view it, and how it influences the space in a room. My ideas are developed through sketches, scale drawings, full-sized drawings, and full-sized mock-ups. I feel it's important to give furniture a more organic form. Except for flat or functional areas, forms, parts, and legs will be rounded, domed, and shaped in some manner. This is to facilitate a crossover relationship between us and the furniture. We are domed and rounded, and all our activities of moving and reaching are in arcs or complex curves.

A few words about technique: It's a given that it has to be flawless, but the real deal is in the design of a piece of furniture. That's what I'm really about. Techniques are just avenues to, or props for, expressing something, and I would like to think a student could see my methods as part of his or her repertoire. The lamination processes I use came out of a design experience and the effort to carry it out. I believe that we furniture designers should design first and then find the appropriate technique to carry it out. If none exists, then invent it.

The designer must not be constrained by technique. Sketches and drawings express important points. The craftsman/designer must find the appropriate technical means to carry them through. I don't generally use carving, inlay, or other surface details. Instead I rely on the strength of the basic form. I feel that the cylinder front desk that I did for the *New American Furniture* exhibition at the Museum of Fine Arts, Boston in 1989 expresses this very well.

My constant challenge is to see exactly what I'm doing—in real time but also with my inner eye. I tend to think in images rather than words. And I try to see in several ways, not only through my eyes and feelings, but also through the eye of a buyer or customer. At the same time I must trust my own focus. My challenge is to get my furniture to express forms from nature: the flow of water, the movement of air, and the growth of trees. This relationship to a more natural form is terribly important to me, but at the same time I do want furniture that is functional.

All the steps in making a piece of furniture are personal to me. They begin with the assignment either from myself or a customer, then the sketches, drawings, development of special jigs, weeks of working, and finally seeing the finished piece.

When I show my slides to students I usually show an incomplete desk, so I can share some of the fun of doing a piece of furniture. The top is off so you can see the structure. It has my usual laminated legs but with an unconventional framing system. It also shows the two small drawers with a curved runner system I developed. It's an in-process look; they probably won't be seen again. When I explain the slide, I don't just see the view; I remember the whole process.

I like going to work every day. Things always seem new in the morning. The time I spend in my workshop is special to me—a time of work or production, yes, but also a time of rejuvenation. It's time of a different sort. I don't notice the hours go by. Involvement with the full-sized drawings is particularly likely to produce this time shift. I relish what I would call "easy time," such as time spent cutting an odd set of curving dovetails that might take three days.

PHOTO © DIANE JAREST

Finally, I have an outline on how to design. Learn to see, and use a sketchbook. Learn to increase sensitivity to all things from small scale to large. Be alert for new forms, patterns, shadows, and colors, and, in the case of furniture, develop a sensitivity to three-dimensional form. Learn to ask yourself, What did I just see or feel? You need to acquire a visual and experiential vocabulary, so you won't be tempted to borrow parts from others. It's a given in my world particularly that we need a feeling for, and an understanding of, wood. Understand it as a living material—you need to know all that it can offer.

JERE OSGOOD
Bubinga Shell Desk, 1985

66 x 30 x 50 inches (167.7 x 76.2 x 127 cm)
Bubinga, pearwood, wenge
PHOTOS © DEAN POWELL
PRIVATE COLLECTION

JERE OSGOOD
Layton Table, 1993

22 x 14 x 24 inches (55.9 x 35.6 x 61 cm)
Claro walnut, ash
PHOTO © DEAN POWELL
PRIVATE COLLECTION

Hands On

Jere Osgood developed his tapered lamination process because he needed a curved and tapered leg for a desk he had designed. Until then, a curving leg would have been made with equal-thickness laminations and band sawed to its tapered profile. Cutting through the glue lines weakens the leg and produces unsightly scarfed glue lines. Jere demonstrates how his jigs enable him to taper each layer prior to laminating the leg.

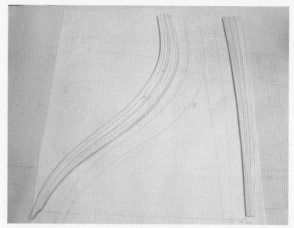

1. The key to the lamination techniques that I use is the thickness-planer jig. For this desk, I needed one double- and one single-taper jig. To make a jig for a leg that tapers toward both ends, the thickest point on the side view of the leg is marked and measured. The ends are measured, too. A flexible ruler measures the length of the laminates required and the distance from one end to the thickest point. Based on the amount of curvature and the flexibility of the stock, I determine how many layers the leg will require and divide each thickness by that number. To keep the math easy, I measure the thicknesses in thousandths, using dial or digital calipers.

2. One piece of ¾-inch MDF is cut to the length and width of the laminate layers. A piece of stiff hardwood is cut to the same size; this piece may need to be thicker. The pieces get glued and screwed together only at the thickest point of the lamination. Then precisely-sized shims are used to move the MDF and produce an even taper. Each shim's thickness is the *difference* between the end thickness and the maximum thickness. More shims are needed

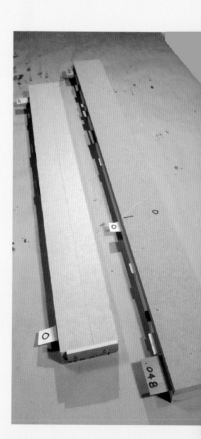

to support the MDF between the thickest point and the ends, but they must not change the curvature attained with the end shims. A jig for a single taper has only one important shim opposite the end that is fastened together. Again, more shims support the MDF between the main shim and the fastened end. A hardwood stop is screwed to the low end of the jig. The stop is used only when band-sawing the balks.

3. I've marked an ash plank to show the trimming cuts.

4. After flattening on the jointer and thicknessing, the planks are ripped to width on the table saw. The resulting balks are 1¾ x 3⅜ x 41 inches.

5. Then one slice is resawed off each balk, using the taper jig against the band-saw fence. The fence is set to cut rough laminates approximately ¹⁄₁₆-inch thicker than the finished laminate.

6. After each pass through the band saw, the face of the balk gets flattened on the jointer.

7. Once all the laminates are sawn from the balks, the laminates are thickness planed to their finished size, again using the taper jig.

8. The arrow on the jig indicates the feed direction through the planer. This is a single-taper jig, and it should be fed with the low end of the jig (the thick end of the laminate) entering first.

9. The thicknesses of the laminate are checked after the first pass through the planer in order to make fine adjustments.

11. Prior to glue-up, paraffin is applied to the edges of the form and the edges of the hardboard cover pieces to make squeezed-out glue easier to clean up.

12. I gather everything needed for gluing up: horses, open glue-up table, heater, thermometer, tarp, and lots of clamps. I use horses with an open frame table so that the heater can warm the laminate while the glue cures.

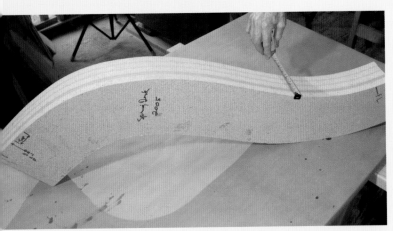

10. The forms for laminating are made from particleboard, chipboard, or MDF—anything without grain direction. The form should be designed to favor the area of a convex bend, as it is harder to push laminates down into a concavity. The taper jig, the gluing form, the laminates, and the cover pieces of hardboard should all be the same width. There should be one piece of hardboard covering the form and then three or four layers on top of the laminate sandwich to distribute the clamp pressure. Allowance is made for the thickness of the hardboard while designing the mold.

13. The area is set up for fast, efficient action. The laminates are stacked in order, to be flipped over as they are glued. The face piece is marked clearly so that it's sure to be placed against the form. A roller is faster than a brush and easily coats all faces within the lamination.

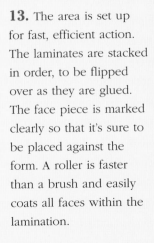

14. I advise using a glue from the urea formaldehyde family. It sets hard, with good cross-linking, resulting in less spring-back than other glues, and has generous working time. I recommend Unibond 800. It is easy to mix, has gap-filling properties, and comes in light, medium, and dark shades. Wear gloves, and don't rinse the excess glue down the sink. It peels pretty easily from plastic tubs and roller pans after it dries.

15. I place the clamps in an alternating pattern, about 3 inches on center, starting at the top and working down to the foot of the leg. The hammer is close at hand for whacking things into alignment—what we call "fine adjustment."

16. Here is the completed glue-up. I set a thermometer on the clamps, cover the whole business with a tarp, and set a heater underneath the open table. I try to maintain an 80° environment inside the tarp and let the glue cure for 24 hours.

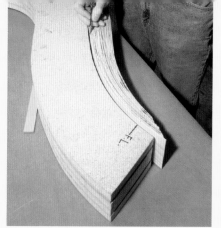

17. There will likely be some spring-back indicating that the laminate tried to straighten.

18. The glued leg needs to be trimmed to width. A pencil line drawn using a thin flexible ruler establishes a straight edge. About ¼ inch gets trimmed off one side. A small clamp holds the ruler.

19. The underside of the leg blank may have glue bumps that need to be trimmed off. Then one side is trimmed by bandsawing freehand. This could be a dangerous cut, so I'm sure to keep my hands in safe positions. The sawn edge gets trued up on the jointer.

20. To trim the blank to width, the line to be sawed is established using a set combination square or a pencil-marking gauge. Note that this leg has a finished width of 2⅝ inches, so the pencil line should be at 2¹¹⁄₁₆ inches to allow for a trip through the thicknesser. Then the second edge is bandsawed.

21. I run the leg through the thicknesser, which I set at 2⅝ inches. The back leg is planed to thickness at the same time.

22. I'm preparing to cut the scarf into the top of the back leg. A piece of vellum is taped over the working drawing, and both legs are traced on the vellum. This step ensures that the joint matches the legs as made, rather than matching the ideal indicated on the drawings.

23. The vellum is cut, and the curve is traced onto the back leg...

24. ...and onto a piece of MDF, which will serve as a shaper template.

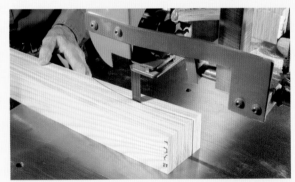

25. The back leg should be cut just outside the line and trimmed to the exact profile, using the MDF template on the shaper with a ball-bearing guide and straight cutters.

26. I mark the layout for the double mortise in the front leg, working directly on the full-sized working drawing. The marking is repeated for the back leg.

27. The double mortises are cut on the mortiser. Note the positioning template (shown in the photo for step 24) that is placed on the mortiser table to align the leg blank. The mortises for both legs are cut at the same height setting.

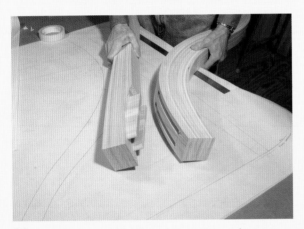

28. After inserting the floating tenons and assembling the legs dry, the legs are checked for accuracy against the full-scale drawing.

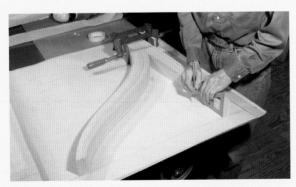

29. The length on the bottoms of the legs is marked and cut, and the ends are sanded. All that's left to finish these legs is to mark their tapers, cut them on the band saw, smooth them, and shape their corners with a spokeshave and rasp. I sand the legs with 50- and 80-grit garnet paper prior to gluing up.

About the Artist

Jere Osgood has been designing and making furniture in his own workshop for more than 40 years. He was named a Fellow of the American Craft Council in 1993 and was given the Award of Distinction by the Furniture Society in 2002, a recognition made more special because it was awarded by his peers. He has shown internationally and is included in many collections, such as the American Craft Museum in New York, the Museum of Fine Arts in Boston, and the Renwick Gallery of the Smithsonian Institution's National Museum of American Art in Washington, D.C.

His education began with architectural school at the University of Illinois and continued at the School for American Craftsmen at Rochester Institute of Technology, where he earned a B.F.A. in 1960. His final year of schooling was spent in an immersion program run by the Scandinavian Seminar in Denmark.

Jere has taught at the Philadelphia College of Art, the School for American Craftsmen, and the Program in Artisanry at Boston University. In regard to his educational practice, he has said many times, "I am not really here teaching you—I'm back in my studio working." He has also conducted many summer workshops at Penland and elsewhere, a practice he has continued during his "retirement."

After publishing three articles on lamination techniques for *Fine Woodworking* in the late '70s, he's left writing about himself to others. Among the many articles published about him, Jere was most impressed with a chapter in Michael Stone's *Contemporary American Woodworkers* (G.M. Smith, 1986) and an interview by Amy Forsyth for *Woodwork* magazine in 2001.

Gallery

All these makers are important to me in some way. Except for David Ebner, Daniel Jackson, and Ted Blachly, they are former students. Some use my lamination techniques in their work, and with others I've just liked the furniture they have been doing over the years. It has been very gratifying to see their names appear in notices of exhibitions or in publications of one kind or another. Here is just a sampling, as there are many more I could cite.

I am pleased to be including work by **Daniel Jackson**. We were at school together in the late '50s. He produced a fair-sized body of work during his short career, but I really feel that his personal connections with people were equally important. He touched a lot of people in very profound ways. There is a clarity in his furniture forms that was distinctly his. The *Library Ladder* and the *Single Music Stand* express his spirit very well. *Sophia's Desk* is important because it displays many aspects of the influence of the Danish craftsman Peder Moos, who was important to both of us.

Thomas Hucker and I have exhibited together several times at Pritam & Eames. We really don't work the same way, but we feel a kinship to each other's work. His *Ebony Oval* is a wonderful form that seems to hover. This is one of two pieces that are almost identical except that one is dark and the other light. Together they play on the changes of our concept of mass. The *Low Table with Bronze* is one of his best—almost a signature piece—with its very sensitive details and exciting juxtaposition of materials.

Of this group I think **Blaise Gaston** has been working longest. He was one of my students in the early '70s at Rochester Institute of Technology. He began in architectural woodworking, but now he makes furniture exclusively. I appreciate the technical virtuosity in these well-designed pieces.

As a student **Michael Hurwitz** did fine work, and he just continues to become better and better. He has developed a refined sense of design. Much of his work is metaphorical, and he expresses his thoughts well in dimensional form.

I have seen a lot of **David Ebner**'s pieces over the years. They are fine works, and I've always felt a great affinity for his furniture. The *Rocking Chair* is one of his best pieces, while the *Bamboo Bench* shows a good new direction.

Stewart Wurtz is also one of my students from our days at Boston University's Program in Artisanry. There is great economy of form in his pieces—clean simple designs all in perfect balance. This economy may or may not carry over into his technique, which is sometimes complex.

I have always liked the approach of **James Schriber**. He has done well by combining fine complex pieces of furniture with simpler pieces and architectural work.

There is so much of **Tim Philbrick** in the *Grecian Sofa*. It shows his classical training, but he has pushed its design further. The legs and rounded shaping are distinctly his details.

Bruce Beeken and **Jeff Parsons** have a great partnership. Bruce is mainly involved with design, and Jeff handles the production. The *Pleissner Chair* and the *Hickory Armchair* are excellent examples of their work together.

Ted Blachly has not been working as long as some of the others but is producing consistently fine work. The *Love Seat* is a wonderful, flowing sculptural form. The *Silver Chest* is another excellent example of his work, with its fine detailing on the drawers and legs. Ted will occasionally help me out in the shop, which is a treat as he is an excellent craftsman.

DANIEL JACKSON
Single Music Stand (Ginko Shaped), 1968

53 inches tall (134.6 cm)
Walnut
PHOTO © CLAIRE KOFSKY
BY PERMISSION OF THE ARTIST'S FAMILY

DANIEL JACKSON
Library Ladder, 1965

72 x 18 inches (182.9 x 45.7 cm)
Walnut, oak
PHOTO © CLAIRE KOFSKY
COLLECTION OF THE RENWICK GALLERY OF THE SMITHSONIAN
AMERICAN ART MUSEUM, WASHINGTON, DC
BY PERMISSION OF THE ARTIST'S FAMILY

DANIEL JACKSON
Sophia's Desk, 1963

50 x 32 x 21 inches (127 x 81.3 x 53.3 cm)
Cherry
PHOTO © CLAIRE KOFSKY
COLLECTION OF JUDY COADY
BY PERMISSION OF THE ARTIST'S FAMILY

THOMAS HUCKER
Low Table with Bronze, 1986

16 x 72 x 18 inches (40.6 x 182.9 x 45.7 cm)
Wenge, patina, cast bronze
PHOTO © ARTIST

THOMAS HUCKER
Ebony Oval, 1991

36 x 72 x 22 inches (91.4 x 182.9 x 55.9 cm)
Maccassar, ebony, black lacquer, maple, silver
PHOTO © ARTIST

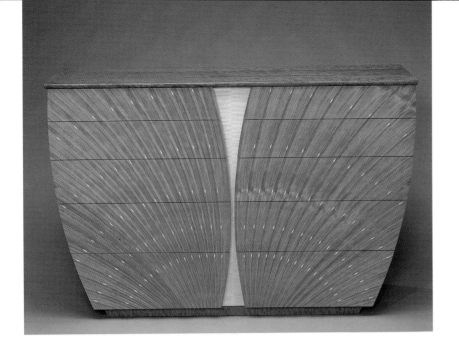

BLAISE GASTON

Lelia's Dresser, 2000

50 x 70 x 20 inches (127 x 177.8 x 50.8 cm)
Bubinga, maple; tapered lamination, veneered
PHOTO © ALAN HOUSEL

BLAISE GASTON

Helios, 2002

16 x 25 x 48 inches (40.6 x 63.5 x 121.9 cm)
Bubinga, copper paint; vacuum-press lamination
PHOTO © PHILIP BEAURLINE

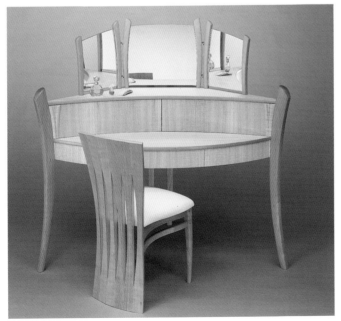

BLAISE GASTON

Untitled, 1996

60 x 50 x 50 inches (152.4 x 127 x 127 cm)
Ash, cherry, brass; curved
PHOTO © PHILIP BEAURLINE

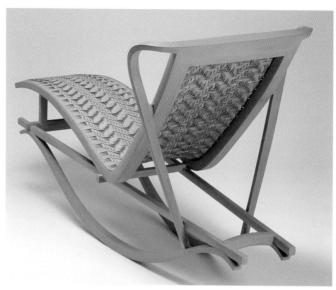

MICHAEL HURWITZ
Dressing Table, 1996

55 x 45 x 21½ inches (139.7 x 114.3 x 54.6 cm)
Ash, copper, silver, marble mosaic
PHOTO © TOM BRUMMETT
COLLECTION OF TAMARA AND BILL PULLMAN

MICHAEL HURWITZ
Rocking Chaise with Leather Seat, 1992

36 x 78 x 30 inches (91.4 x 198.1 x 76.2 cm)
Walnut, leather; laminated, woven, painted
PHOTO © TOM BRUMMETT

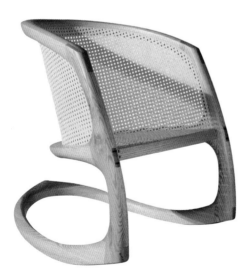

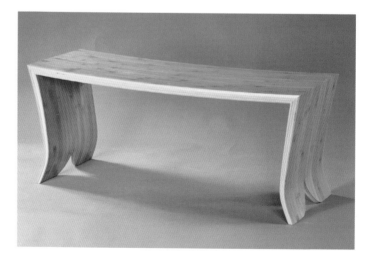

DAVID N. EBNER
Rocking Chair, 1995

30 x 28 x 30 inches (76.2 x 71.1 x 76.2 cm)
Red oak and cane, oil finish; stacked, carved,
cold-bent lamination
PHOTO © GIL AND STEPHEN AMIAGA
COURTESY OF MODERNE GALLERY, PHILADELPHIA, PA

DAVID N. EBNER
Bamboo Bench I, 2003

16½ x 42 x 14 inches (41.9 x 106.7 x 35.6 cm)
Amber bamboo, lauan core; tapered, vacuum
pressed, lacquered
PHOTO © GIL AND STEPHEN AMIAGA
COURTESY OF PRITAM & EAMES

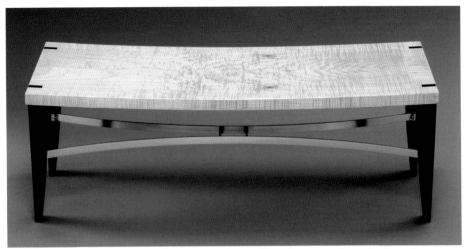

STEWART WURTZ

Rubin Bench, 2002

17 x 48 x 20 inches
(43.2 x 121.9 x 50.8 cm)
Big leaf maple, wenge, stainless steel;
veneered, laminated
PHOTO © GREG DIANICH

STEWART WURTZ

Lacewood Desk, 2005

29 x 72 x 32 inches (73.7 x 182.9 x 81.3 cm)
Lacewood, wenge, maple; bent lamination, mortise and
tenon joinery, dovetailed
PHOTO © ROBERT MCCRORY

STEWART WURTZ

Desk 95, 1995

34½ x 60 x 26 inches (87.6 x 152.4 x 66 cm)
Cherry, curly maple, ebony, sterling silver; veneered, bent
lamination, dovetailed
PHOTO © TERRY REED

JAMES SCHRIBER
*"Deuce" Game Table
with Chairs,* 2005

Table, 28 x 29 x 29 inches (71.1 x 73.7 x 73.7 cm);
each chair, 30 x 20 x 22 inches (76.2 x 50.8 x 55.9 cm)
Curly maple; ebonized
PHOTO © JOHN KANE

JAMES SCHRIBER
Big Chair with Ottoman, 2004

Chair, 43 x 27 x 29 inches (109.2 x 68.6 x 73.7 cm);
ottoman, 15 x 23 inches (38.1 x 58.4 cm)
Bubinga, mohair
PHOTO © JOHN KANE
COURTESY OF PRITAM & EAMES

TIMOTHY S. PHILBRICK
Secretary, 2003

98 x 44 x 24 inches (248.9 x 111.8 x 61 cm)
Cuban mahogany
PHOTOS © KAREN PHILIPPI
PRIVATE COLLECTION

TIMOTHY S. PHILBRICK
Grecian Sofa, 2000

31 x 66 x 24 inches (78.7 x 167.6 x 61 cm)
Curly maple, silk fabric
PHOTO © RIC MURRAY
COURTESY OF PETER JOSEPH GALLERY, NEW YORK, NY

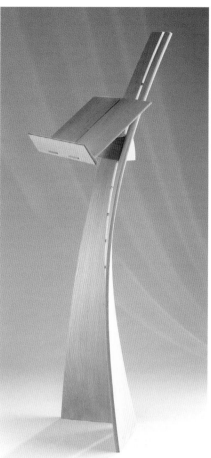

BEEKEN PARSONS
Music Stand, 1989

60 x 24 x 20 inches (152.4 x 61 x 50.8 cm)
White oak; steam bent
PHOTO © DIDIER DELMAS

BEEKEN PARSONS
Hickory Armchair, 1991

31 x 18 x 18 inches (78.7 x 45.7 x 45.7 cm)
Hickory, hickory splint; steam bent
PHOTO © SANDERS MILENS

BEEKEN PARSONS
Pleissner Chair, 1996

36 x 40 x 24 inches (91.4 x 101.6 x 61 cm)
Hickory, leather; steam bent
PHOTO © SANDERS MILENS

TED BLACHLY
Silver Chest, 2002

34 x 38 x 19 inches (86.4 x 96.5 x 48.3 cm)
Curly sugar maple, aged cherry, varnish
PHOTO © DEAN POWELL
PRIVATE COLLECTION

TED BLACHLY
Love Seat, 2005

31 x 54 x 26 inches (78.7 x 137.2 x 66 cm)
Curly sugar maple, varnish
PHOTO © DEAN POWELL

Jenna Goldberg

 Because Jenna Goldberg is convinced that every cabinet should hold a secret and a surprise, you won't be able to guess what's inside one of her armoires before you open the doors. The intricate patterns she paints and carves enliven the surfaces of her furniture, but they also establish an expectation of wonders stored within. Jenna reveals the connections between shoes, furniture, and people before demonstrating her methods for attaining layered, intriguing patterns on her cabinets.

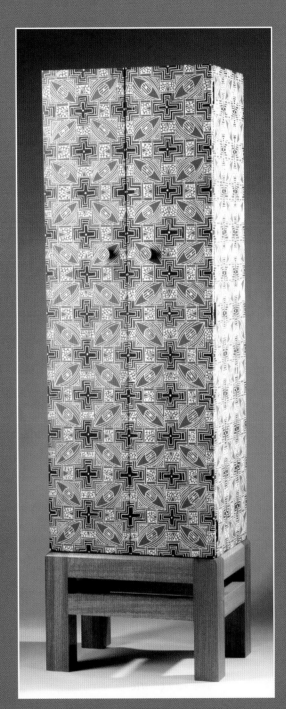
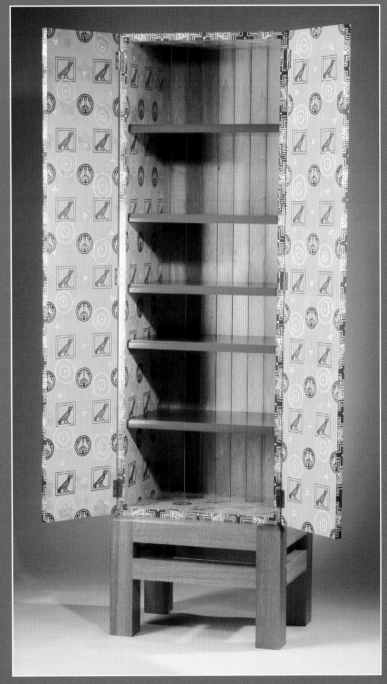

JENNA GOLDBERG
Cooke Cabinet, 2005

84 x 17 x 24 inches (213.4 x 43.2 x 61 cm)
Basswood, paint; carved

Of Shoes and Patterns

Like most kids, I read *The Lion, the Witch and the Wardrobe*. The metaphor of entering another world through the secret portal of a wardrobe fascinated me as a child and still fascinates me today. At a young age, the fantastic imagery prompted me to think of my furniture in a different way. My friends and I would constantly rearrange my bedroom with precariously stacked furniture attached by stretched blankets and sheets. Much to my mother's displeasure, my bedroom always looked like a refugee camp. I found the little closed spaces comforting, and my young mind hoped to discover some secret and special world there.

I grew up in a family of artists, which was apparent to anyone who visited our modest suburban home. Amazingly, my parents managed to

JENNA GOLDBERG
Ginko Buffet, 2005

38 x 60 x 18 inches (96.5 x 152.4 x 45.7 cm)
Cherry, maple, paint; carved
PHOTO © MARK JOHNSTON
PRIVATE COLLECTION

cram little art studios into every corner of our house. My dad had his pottery studio, his woodshop, a darkroom, and a little corner in which he'd experiment with enameling. My mother worked with batik and had a fabric studio. As children, my brother and I would travel with my parents to craft fairs up and down the East Coast. This was high adventure when I was young. It was also my introduction to a lifestyle that I later came to adopt for myself.

When I was about 10, my mother taught me to sew, and I spent many afternoons trying to figure out how to design and make my own handbags, eyeglass cases—whatever I could dream up. I was resistant to following sewing patterns. To this day, I don't like to follow a recipe, directions, or plans. I would rather try to figure it out myself.

I have always loved shoes. From the time I could hold a pair of scissors, I would cut soles for my creations out of cardboard. I would sift through my mother's piles of patterned fabrics in search of the perfect design. My parents always thought I'd become a shoe designer, and for a while so did I, but for now I'm a shoe consumer. I can't make it through Nordstrom without at least a quick visit to the shoe department. It's so easy to spot the perfect heel, the beautiful soft leather or funky faux furs, the fine details in the stitching. What draws me to shoes is fundamentally the same aesthetic that attracts me to furniture. I love the fact that both shoes and furniture can run the gamut from the banal to the ridiculous, from the practical to the funky. People reveal much about themselves by what they choose to put on their feet, just as they do by the way they furnish their homes.

My family loved to collect antiques and junk, so it was only natural for me to start haunting the junk shops and auction houses when I was in college. I didn't know what I was looking for, but I knew it when I saw it. I collected old photos and boxes of letters that illuminated the histories of strangers. I used the old photos as inspiration for my work. An

Jenna Goldberg

JENNA GOLDBERG
Cherry Blossom Armoire, 2005

75 x 44 x 24 inches (190.5 x 111.8 x 61 cm)
Mahogany, maple, paint; carved, screen-printed, hand-painted
PHOTOS © MARK JOHNSTON
PRIVATE COLLECTION

JENNA GOLDBERG
Fiona's Toy Chest, 2002

20 x 44 x 22 inches (50.8 x 111.8 x 55.9 cm)
Poplar, maple, paint; carved
PHOTO © MARK JOHNSTON
PRIVATE COLLECTION

old wedding photo made it into one piece. Once, I felt compelled to join the portraits of two people who looked good together. They are forever linked in some ersatz history. Not surprisingly, my quest for the perfect collectibles left me with an inventory of disparate items in need of a home. Sheer pragmatism has certainly been one of the reasons I'm drawn to designing cabinets and wardrobes.

My undergraduate training as an illustrator allowed me to convey stories and ideas through imagery. I enjoyed working two-dimensionally, until I took a beginning woodworking course during my junior year. The process of making furniture came very naturally, and I was seduced by the ability to handle and manipulate the materials. When I would come home from college, I would sit in the living room for hours looking through my father's *Fine Woodworking* and *Fine Homebuilding* magazines. These magazines got me thinking about changing

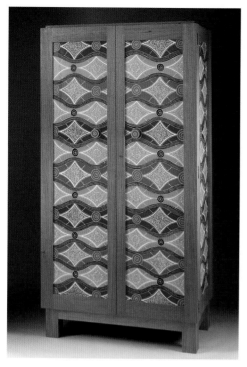

JENNA GOLDBERG
Matchbox Armoire, 2004

75 x 44 x 22 inches (190.5 x 111.8 x 55.9 cm)
Mahogany, maple, paint; carved
PHOTOS © MARK JOHNSTON
PRIVATE COLLECTION

the focus of my studies. I chose to switch my emphasis to furniture making but decided to do it after getting my B.F.A. in illustration.

After graduating I immediately set up shop in my mother's garage. Armed with some crusty old tools and a few clamps, I started making small pieces that I could add to a portfolio. My intention was to find a furniture program to hone my skills. This search led me to attend many different programs including the Genoa School, San Diego State University's graduate program in furniture, and ultimately the graduate program in furniture design at RISD.

My intent when I first started making furniture was to make pieces that people would save as heirlooms. I could only hope that future generations would feel lucky to inherit one of my pieces. I did not want to make traditional pieces per se, but to make pieces that were timeless, well made, and unique. Furniture has intimacy, and for me it holds an emotional charge. I am fascinated by the story of the chair purchased at a yard sale that is now a collectible, or the dresser that had a piece of lace

on it for so many years that its pattern got burned into the surface. I still have my great grandmother's bedroom set, and, although it is not to my taste, it carries with it a history that is meaningful to me. With my furniture I hope to evoke memories and emotions through the colors and images, and through the stories that happen during its lifetime.

My fascination with pattern came to me at an early age. When I was nine, my parents took my brother and me to Greece and Israel. This was the first time I experienced ruins and what the word "old" really means. Everywhere you go in Israel, there is an overlapping of cultures, religions, and holy sites. It is not uncommon to find mosques, churches, and temples built on top of each other. In both temples and mosques, the ornamentation is done mostly with geometric pattern. It is considered blasphemous to use images of people or animals in either place of worship, as it is feared that this could lead to idolatry or the belief in multiple gods.

When I returned for my last two years of high school, the Middle East nurtured my fascination with Islamic architecture and pattern. These patterns, based on geometry, logic, and order, express a vision of the universe that is at once abstract and infinite. Incorporating pattern into a structure was thought to beautify the space and organize the environment so as to elevate one spiritually.

I embrace this concept of pattern in my own work. While I draw from many different places, images, and concepts, I still want to be able to organize imagery into one cohesive piece. When images and colors compete in my work, the carved patterns provide unity and harmony.

All my furniture pieces are one-of-a-kind, but my process is fairly consistent. First, I assemble a palette of colors. I habitually grab handfuls of color swatches whenever I'm in the paint

JENNA GOLDBERG
Rose Dresser, 2003

65 x 44 x 22 inches
(165.1 x 111.8 x 55.9 cm)
Mahogany, maple, paint; carved
PHOTO © MARK JOHNSTON
PRIVATE COLLECTION

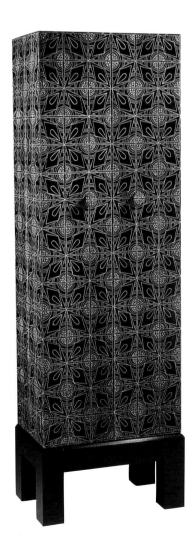

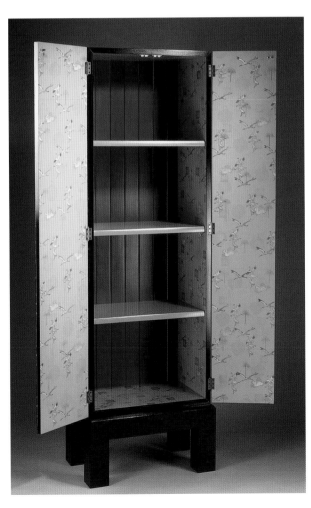

JENNA GOLDBERG
Samba Cabinet, 2004

80 x 24 x 14 inches
(203.2 x 61 x 35.6 cm)
Walnut, paint; carved
PHOTOS © MARK JOHNSTON
PRIVATE COLLECTION

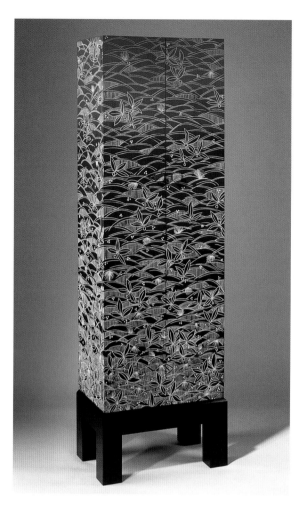

JENNA GOLDBERG
Falling Leaves, 2004

75 x 24 x 16 inches (190.5 x 61 x 40.6 cm)
Basswood, paint; carved
PHOTO © MARK JOHNSTON
COLLECTION OF THE RENWICK GALLERY OF THE SMITHSONIAN
AMERICAN ART MUSEUM, WASHINGTON, DC

or hardware store. Sometimes I cut colors or scenes from magazines to get a feel for color values and contrasts. The patterns on the outsides of my cabinets tend to be very organized, formal, and almost stoic. They are composed primarily of carved lines confined to a tight grid system. The insides of my cabinets feel much lighter. Evocative imagery abounds on these interiors. I find these images everywhere—in stamps or the stacks of illustrations in my studio that—much like the orphaned photographs I used in my earlier work—lie waiting to be cast in a furniture dialogue. I see my cabinets as having lives, almost as though they were people. They are always different on the inside, much like people are.

I approach the making of furniture with a bit of abandon. While I value my firm grasp on most things technical, I sometimes like surrendering a bit of that control to experimentation, especially when it comes to the surface decoration. I learn more by not knowing exactly what the outcome of the piece will be. This element of surprise gives a piece of furniture more energy.

Juxtaposing a variety of images leaves a great deal to interpretation. I will try several ideas on scrap boards until I get the right feeling or look. I find it necessary to do practice boards. They provide opportunities to take chances and make mistakes and also to discover something unforeseen. They also serve as inspiration for future projects.

The cabinet, more than any other piece of furniture, appeals to me because of the anticipation one feels when opening its doors. I envision my cabinetry as reliquaries for collections, a home for one's objects of desire, a place to store memories. Often my decorations or carvings are reflective of the objects that the cabinet may contain, or reminiscent of the feelings one might have when interacting with the collection. My aim is to recall these memories and emotions through the sensory experience of simply opening the doors.

Hands On

Jenna Goldberg has developed a process of painting, block and screen printing, and carving wooden panels to achieve lively surfaces on her chests, cabinets, and other furniture. She directs the layering of information by using grids that respond to the scale of the piece and to the motifs she intends to use. Here Jenna demonstrates making the grid and using it to produce a patterned surface.

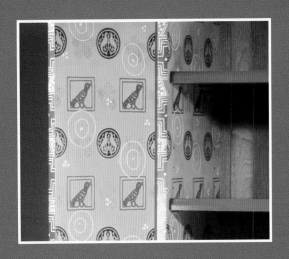

1. Mixing ample amounts of all colors needed for the project helps to avoid having to remix more paint later. It's a good idea to write all the colors used in the mix on the container itself.

2. I label the mixed paint with the parts it will be used for (e.g. cabinet doors) and with the project/client's name. This way, if there are several projects going on at once, the paints won't get confused.

3. The top and inside edges of the doors have been labeled with a pencil. I paint the entire surface with the mixed paint. The brush strokes should go in the same direction as the grain of the wood. I usually do three layers, allowing each coat to dry fully before applying the next. The first and second layers don't need sanding between coats.

4. After the second layer has dried, the surface is lightly sanded, and the dust is wiped off gently with a tack cloth. Then the third coat of paint is applied. Tack cloths should not be left sitting on a finished surface because the tacky surface can stain your wood or paint.

Jenna Goldberg

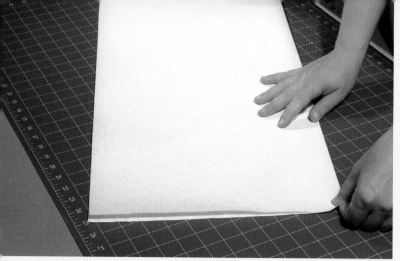

8. I mark those center registration lines in red or another bold color.

5. To make a template for the silk screens, a sheet of paper is cut to the size of the two doors put together. It is folded in half both ways to find the center points, and a notch is cut at the centerline of each edge to make the lines easier to see.

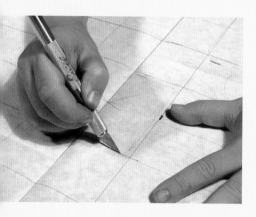

6. A ruler and triangle help to construct a grid that will perfectly fit in the space available. The grid can be any configuration. I know the silk screens I am going to be working with are 5 x 7 inches, so I make my rectangles that size. Once the grid of 5 x 7-inch rectangles is drawn on the paper, the centerlines of those rectangles can be marked. These lines will be the registration marks that will later match up with the centerlines of the silk screens. The lines run all the way across the paper.

9. The paper grid is laid out over the two doors that will be printed, matching up the centerlines. The top side should be marked. The paper should be taped down firmly.

7. Then the rectangles are cut out. These cuts do not need to be perfect, and it is better to cut about ½ inch in from the line. This way, when the screens lie on the grid, the registration marks will overlap the paper without blocking the screen area.

10. Blue masking tape (my favorite, because it doesn't leave any tacky residue on my wood or painted surface) marks where the screen prints will go. This makes a loose grid to show where to print with the rubber stamp. The blue tape now acts as a reminder of where not to stamp.

Jenna Goldberg

11. A variety of stamps and colors for the piece may be picked out ahead of time.

12. I am fairly loose about this part. I will start with one stamp and one color and print perhaps in the left bottom corner of the squares between the blue tape marks. Then, with another stamp and color, I may print on the top right side of the square and so on.

13. I do this until I feel that the density of the stamp pattern is satisfactory. This part can go quickly. When the stamping is done, the blue tape is removed.

14. To make my screens I use the Print Gocco machine, an easy way to make silk screens from a black-and-white photocopy. The cardboard frame should be covered with clear packing tape to keep it dry during clean up.

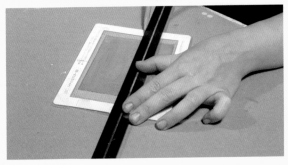

15. The centerlines of the image are marked on the screen frame. The image may not be centered on the screen, so the edges of the image are marked, and those marks are used to find the centerlines. These will be the registration marks.

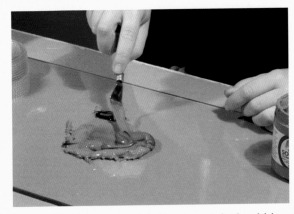

16. An ample amount of silk-screen ink should be mixed. I like the water-based acrylic inks. An artist's spatula can be used to mix the paint on a piece of glass. When the ink's mixed, it stays in an airtight container marked with the project name.

screen with a damp (not soaking) sponge. With each wipe the screen goes on a new page of the phone book. A slightly damp paper towel should be fine for cleaning the back of the screen. You must be careful when cleaning the back, as the emulsion can be fragile.

17. Now the paper grid goes back on the wood, with the top pointing in the right direction and the centerlines where they should be. Again, the grid gets taped firmly to the boards.

The screen is placed in the first square with the registration marks on the screen frame matched up with the centerlines/registration marks on the paper grid. I like to start at the top and work my way down the board, so I don't smear the ink as I go. A generous amount of ink lies at the top of the screen just above where the image starts. Using a good sturdy squeegee and starting from the top, I squeegee enough ink over the screen to cover the whole image. I do two passes in one direction and then one in the opposite direction, returning all the ink from the bottom of the screen back up to the top.

20. When all the openings in the grid have been printed, it can be removed from the work. Now the paper grid (A) is used to make another paper grid (B) to print between the grid (A) squares.

18. The photo at right shows the first few prints.

21. With paper grid (A) lying over paper grid (B), an X is drawn from the corners of the rectangles on grid (A) in order to find the center points of the areas between the openings. The center is marked using a center punch or awl. These points will be the centers of the openings for grid (B). Again, centerlines are drawn on grid (B) to provide registration marks for the new screen. A new image prints in the spaces between those of the first set.

19. An old phone book comes in handy for cleaning up the screen. Paper towels will eliminate a majority of the ink on the front of the screen. Then, the remaining ink can be wiped from the

Jenna Goldberg

22. If there's an image that will hang over an edge, a board the same thickness as the printed board can be laid flush against the painted board. This will provide for equal squeegee pressure on both sides of the screen.

23. Oops! Sometimes the prints don't come out as well as you'd like. I use a fine brush and the same paint to fill in where the image seems blotchy. Several coats may be needed to equal the printed opacity.

24. Wearing a respirator and gloves, I use a foam brush to apply a layer of gel varnish. I work in a ventilated area, and leave the room after each coat. The first layer can look streaky, but the second and third layers will even it all out. Two coats are applied first, leaving about six to eight hours of drying time in between. Then the varnish is sanded lightly with 220-grit sandpaper. A tack cloth removes all the dust after sanding. Then one more coat goes on.

25. Now the pieces are ready for carving. My preferred tools are an 11/4 (#11 curve, 4-mm wide) veiner and a 7/14 veiner. The #11 is a deep-scoop veiner—the deepest curve you can get before going into V-gouges. It is great for doing linear work. The tool's sharpness can be tested on a scrap piece of wood. The veiner should be able to cut across the grain without tearing.

26. First I mark the panel with blue tape where I want to carve my circles. That way I can make sure they are spaced equally and in a pleasing manner before I start carving.

27. This carving technique works on the pull stroke. Beginners should carve in ½-inch strokes, connecting all the lines until the correct shape is completed. The longer strokes that experience and confidence bring make the work go more smoothly.

28. After I have carved all my big circles, I go back in and carve the smaller inside circles. Sometimes turning the board or turning oneself are necessary to carve a complete circle.

29. After my circles are finished, I use the blue tape to mark where my dots will go.

30. When making the dots, I move the tool across the grain in a flicking motion. If you go with the grain, your dot tends to become a line. You have much more control over the shape of the dot when you are carving across the grain. This technique can take years of practice, but it's worth the work.

About the Artist

After growing up between the Hudson River and Connecticut, Jenna Goldberg spent her last two years of high school studying in Israel. The patterns of the Middle East became enduring design inspirations for her. With an undergraduate degree in illustration and a little tutoring in woodworking, she went to Rhode Island School of Design to earn an M.F.A. in furniture design. She has since maintained her own studio in Providence, Rhode Island, except for a five-year period spent in Asheville, North Carolina.

She mounted her first solo show at Gallery NAGA in 1996, and has had shows in various other galleries, including John Elder, Pritam & Eames, and Clark Gallery. Her work is represented in the collections of the Renwick Gallery of the Smithsonian American Art Museum and the Mint Museum of Craft + Design. Her furniture has also found place in significant private collections, including those of Ron Abramson, Sam Maloof, and Stephen King.

In addition to her full-time studio furniture practice, Jenna teaches part-time at RISD and offers workshops at Penland and other schools.

Gallery

There are so many artists and craftsmen who have inspired me over the years; I wish I could pay homage to them all. The artists I have chosen for this gallery section are those whose work I have admired and lusted after throughout my career. They all seem to have the ability to tell a story through their work.

I was lucky enough to take a workshop with **Kristina Madsen** back in 1994. It was in this class that I learned how to do intaglio carving. Kristina learned this technique while on a Fulbright in Fiji. Although inspired by the traditional carvings of the South Pacific, she uniquely combines classic design with her own brand of flowing, carved patterns. Her work is beautiful, flawless, and powerful.

I first came to know **Wendy Maruyama** in 1992 when I signed on as one of her graduate students at San Diego State University (due to an unfortunate turn of events, I left after one semester to finish my studies at RISD). Wendy's bold use of form, color, and carving has always inspired me. I truly admire her ability to blend images from pop culture and tradition in satirical ways. Her work has influenced me in so many ways. I am thankful that my family lives in the same city as she does, and that I've been able to see her, stay current with her work, and maintain our friendship.

I was first introduced to the work of **Alphonse Mattia** when I was an undergrad studying illustration. Michael Hurwitz, my elective woodworking teacher at the time, told me to go see slides of Alphonse's work. It made me sit up and take notice. It was the first time I realized furniture didn't have to be brown and square. Alphonse's work conveys the narrative and illustrative side of furniture making. I've always appreciated his knack for form, craftsmanship and most of all, his ability to combine it successfully with his biting wit.

Judy Kensley McKie's work makes me want to win the lottery. She is inspired by African, Indonesian, and other styles of indigenous design, as well as by the Moderne design of the 1930s. Her animal work is wonderfully playful, illustrative, and streamlined. I admire her for being able to make it look so simple. Lord knows, it is anything but simple.

Bobby Hansson's work appeals to the junk hoarder in me. He has a unique ability to look at an object and see something else in it. Consisting of sculpture, furniture, and musical instruments, his work usually culminates in an object that has some sort of quirky story or narrative. I think he is great!

KRISTINA MADSEN
Chest on Stand, 1995
33½ x 33 x 13 inches
(85.1 x 83.8 x 33 cm)
Chakte kok, padauk
PHOTOS © DAVID STANSBURY

KRISTINA MADSEN

Cabinet on Stand, 1999

61 x 26 x 14 inches
(154.9 x 66 x 35.6 cm)
Sucupira, dyed pearwood veneer
over maple and imbuya
PHOTOS © DAVID STANSBURY

KRISTINA MADSEN

Chest of Drawers, 1996

60 x 40 x 20 inches (152.4 x 101.6 x 50.8 cm)
Pearwood, gesso
PHOTOS © DAVID STANSBURY

KRISTINA MADSEN

Blanket Chest, 1995

23½ x 51 x 15 inches (59.7 x 129.5 x 38.1 cm)
Dyed pearwood veneer over maple, wenge
PHOTO © DAVID STANSBURY

WENDY MARUYAMA
Box on Stand, 1988

36 x 20 x 20 inches (91.4 x 50.8 x 50.8 cm)
Polychromed and carved basswood
PHOTO © CARY OKAZAKI

WENDY MARUYAMA
Patterned Chest Series, 1990

18 x 45 x 15 inches (45.7 x 114.3 x 38.1 cm)
Polychromed basswood
PHOTO © CARY OKAZAKI

ALPHONSE MATTIA
Fetish Too, 2005

40 x 42 x 36 inches
(101.6 x 106.7 x 91.4 cm)
Bubinga, fabric, lacquer;
carved, shaped
PHOTO © ERIC GOULD

ALPHONSE MATTIA
The Precarious Balance of Time, 2002

82 x 16 x 16 inches (208.3 x 40.6 x 40.6 cm)
Russian plywood, English brown oak veneer,
pau amarillo, curly maple, assorted hardwoods,
paint, stain, pigment, lacquer
PHOTO © MARK JOHNSTON

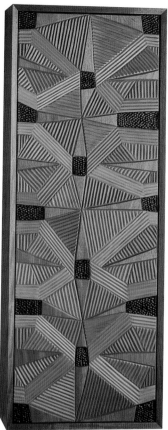

JUDY KENSLEY MCKIE
Pointing Cabinet, 2002

50½ x 19½ x 5¼ inches (128.3 x 49.5 x 13.3 cm)
Mahogany, paint; carved
PHOTO © DEAN POWELL

JUDY KENSLEY MCKIE
Tall Black Cabinet, 1987

86 x 23 x 11 inches
(218.4 x 58.4 x 27.9 cm)
Limewood, milk paint; carved
PHOTO © DAVID CARAS

JUDY KENSLEY MCKIE
Ivory Couch, 2003

36 x 64 x 28 inches
(91.4 x 162.6 x 71.1 cm)
Resin, mohair; cast
PHOTO © SCOTT MCCUE

Jenna Goldberg

BOBBY HANSSON
Celestial Throne for Nevelson, 1988

Found wood, spray paint, nails
PHOTO © ARTIST

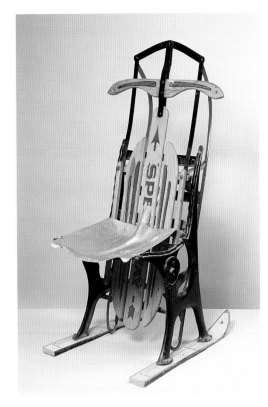

BOBBY HANSSON
Throne for the Snow Queen

Sled, shovel, skis, school desk
PHOTO © ARTIST

BOBBY HANSSON
Yin Yang Chair

Chairs, map stand, spray paint
PHOTO © ARTIST

BOBBY HANSSON
Viking Throne

Wood; hand adzed with
forged iron axe
PHOTO © ARTIST
COLLECTION OF CRAIG NUTT

Jenna Goldberg

John Clark

The excellent craftsmanship displayed in John Clark's furniture corresponds with the attentive care with which he treats his studio. Not only do the tools and equipment have their own places, but each is sharp and tuned for its job. Dust has been banished from the premises, helped along by a nearly silent collection system and subtle details in the building itself that contribute to making it an inviting place to work. With the same attention to detail, he demonstrates techniques for achieving fine results with fitting veneers and inlays.

JOHN CLARK
Moon Book Case, 2003
55 x 48 x 14 inches (139.7 x 121.9 x 35.6 cm)
Mahogany, bird's-eye maple, ebony, rosewood

Paying Close Attention

The allure of veneer springs from its inherent beauty, whether it's the flashy seductive radiance of birdseye maple or the voluptuous landscape of quilted makore. Veneer logs are the cream of the sawmill crop. They are often separated from the mundane lumber stock immediately after felling, when the discriminating logger recognizes that he has stumbled upon a treasure. They eventually become part of a magnificent palette from which a furniture maker can choose to create colorful and complex pictures on the surfaces of tables, chests, or cabinets. For a functional furniture maker like me, veneers offer options of color, richness, and even the illusion of texture that can transform an ordinary piece into an exceptional one.

Veneer as a surface, like paint or texture, has a long history in the adornment of furniture. Veneer capitalizes on the natural beauty of the wood but is not limited to it. The complex use of mosaics, marquetry, dyeing, burning, or the incorporation of inlay can all take the veneered surface to higher levels of inventiveness and sophistication. Inlays accentuate and define the borders of contrasting veneers, while their intersections may be punctuated with precious metals or decorative bits of shell.

Throughout the history of furniture, details have determined the success of a design, and the craftsmanship with which those details are executed has determined which pieces find their way into our public and private collections. Cabriole legs, sharkskin, milk paint, marble, bent laminations: the possibilities have been plentiful and the imaginative use of new materials and techniques continues to influence the evolution of studio furniture. I use many of them to try to make my work distinctive and satisfying, but in the end, the craftsmanship element is usually the overriding factor in any decision about what material I use or how I use it. If a piece of handmade furniture falls short in its craftsmanship, no degree of cleverness in its design or presentation can make up for it. I believe the

JOHN CLARK
Corner China Cabinet, 1992

85 x 34 x 26 inches (215.9 x 86.4 x 66 cm)
Plum pudding mahogany, ebony, curly maple;
veneered bent lamination
PHOTO © TOM JOYNT

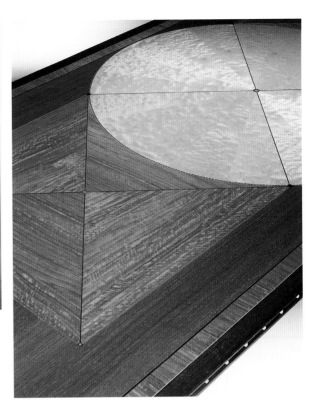

JOHN CLARK
Conference Table, 1993

30 x 50 x 120 inches (76.2 x 127 x 304.8 cm)
Mahogany, coachwood, quilted maple, mother-of-pearl, MDF; veneered, inlaid
PHOTOS © TOM JOYNT

value of my furniture derives from its ability to stand apart from mass-produced pieces, not only for its aesthetic appeal, but also for the care with which it was made. I will never be able to make furniture that is cheaper than what is available from a factory, but I can always make it better.

Because the kind of pieces I make require so much time in advance planning and construction, I don't have much opportunity for experimentation or improvisation during the building process. Occasionally, I will change course on a speculative piece that I am making for sale through a gallery if I find that it is not turning out the way I had hoped. This usually requires a substantial amount of lost time in backtracking or redoing and can be frustrating. I have to be really dissatisfied with that part of the piece before I resort to changing it in midstream, but I rarely regret doing so once I've made the decision to change it.

Mock-ups, models, and samples are some of the methods I use to explore new technical or aesthetic ideas. Of these, I use samples most often, and I find them very helpful as a relatively quick way to try out new materials, techniques, and especially finishing alternatives. Though they can take a while to make and examine, the results are usually well

JOHN CLARK
Side Tables, 1988

25 x 19 x 19 inches (63.5 x 48.3 x 48.3 cm)
Left, curly ash with purpleheart; right, walnut with rosewood; veneered, inlaid
PHOTO © DEAN POWELL

JOHN CLARK
Mignon Dining Table, 1995

30 x 60 x 96 inches (76.2 x 152.4 x 243.8 cm)
Mahogany, wenge, curly ash, MDF; veneered, inlaid
PHOTOS © TOM MILLS

construction. While I have come to rely on them for most quick reference needs, they are not a substitute for the clarity and details that a full-scale drawing provides.

My history as a furniture designer/maker began with my determination, even as a teenager, to tailor the mechanical and aesthetic objects in my life to suit my judgment of the way things should be. I can somehow justify the time it takes to modify the controls on my slot mortiser just because I prefer the switch to be a little higher where it feels right. I don't see the original as being right or wrong, only that the changed position works better for me. In much the same way, I have some built-in sense that the shape of a table's leg might need to have a tighter radius or a different arc in its foot before it becomes my own. I like to think that, to some degree, everyone has an internal preference barometer that determines his or her personal taste. Some of us have an eagerness to make things our own that exceeds practicality, while others are able to tolerate larger deviations of what we can live with.

worth the effort. Similarly, full-scale drawings are a sure way to avoid many surprises that may otherwise arise during the construction. The relationships of joints and intersections of components are often hidden from me until I lay them out life-sized on paper. Even a partial full-scale drawing will reveal discrepancies in construction or proportion that I may not see in a smaller drawing. I have used various computer-aided design or architectural drawing programs to produce accurately scaled working drawings for use in the studio during

JOHN CLARK
Bedside Table, 1999

28 x 22 x 19 inches (71.1 x 55.9 x 48.3 cm)
Mahogany, curly ash, fountainhead, plywood;
veneered
PHOTO © JOHN WARNER

JOHN CLARK
Conference Table & Credenza, 2003

30 x 48 x 72 inches (76.2 x 121.9 x 182.9 cm)
Cherry, quilted maple, quilted makore, MDF; veneered, inlaid
PHOTO © TIM BARNWELL

JOHN CLARK
Moon Dining Table & Chairs, 2001

30 x 72 x 96 inches (76.2 x 182.9 x 243.8 cm)
Mahogany, quilted maple, ebony, rosewood-veneered MDF; inlaid
PHOTOS © ROBERT CUTTER

There is a general perception that people who appear to spend a lot of time and effort fretting over details are obsessed with perfection. I believe it is simply a matter of paying attention coupled with the patience to see the goal realized. When I cut out a template for a veneer sketchface with a router, I focus on the settings that will make that template be the right size for the next step. The template doesn't have to be perfect; it just needs to get the job done. Of course there are times when that passion for getting all the fine points right can derail productivity, and the project can seem to take forever. But when I can keep my concern for the small things from overwhelming the original idea, I consider the piece successful. Ideally, the details will complement the complete design, not overshadow it.

JOHN CLARK
Moon Game Table, 2002

30 x 48 inches (76.2 x 121.9 cm)
Mahogany, rosewood, maple, ebony-veneered MDF;
inlaid, bent lamination
PHOTO © TIM BARNWELL

It has been said that the difference between a craftsperson and a good craftsperson is that the good craftsperson fixes his/her mistakes. While that simplified definition is a good start to understanding the hallmarks of craftsmanship, I look beyond it to an innate need for quality that drives my desire to make things well. No matter how thorough the planning and preparation, there will always be mistakes made, and unanticipated problems will arise during the process of building a piece of furniture. In the end, the level of craftsmanship that piece displays is determined by how far the builder was willing to go to remedy those inevitable setbacks. A decision to backtrack and correct a problem is often as hard as the original design decisions were before the first construction steps were undertaken. It seems that I am forever questioning whether it is worth backtracking and repairing a mismatched joint or a blemish in the finish. I can't recall ever having felt bad about taking the time to patch up a mistake in my furniture, but I will never forget the small repairs I have ignored or dismissed as unnecessary at the time.

Throughout the first 15 years of my furniture-making experience, I worked in a variety of shared shop situations ranging from school workshops to joint ventures with studio partners. I enjoyed the camaraderie and economy of those working environments, and I heartily recommend that kind of situation to anyone who could benefit from the aesthetic stimulus, the busyness of shared activity, and always having an available helping hand. In 1994, I finally had the opportunity and had accumulated enough resources to build my own space, and I was feeling a need for more independence. This new space has become my most productive and satisfying tool, even though I sometimes miss those advantages of a shared shop. Everything in the studio can be tailored to meet the needs of the piece I am working on, and I have the freedom to change my working conditions when necessary. Now I employ a personal mix of tools and equipment that are right for the way I work. The space itself is roomy, open, and airy with good light, all of which makes it an inviting and pleasant place to be. The larger value of working in a tailored environment is its subtle influence on my working confidence and effectiveness.

Hands On

John Clark's flawless craftsmanship allows the exotic materials in his furniture to dance in their intersecting patterns. Here he demonstrates the use of router templates and precise work habits to enliven a surface with veneer and inlay. This demonstration of how he fits the tangentially aligned circle and rectangle on this relatively simple bookcase top reveals some of the strategies he uses to veneer his more complicated pieces.

1. A set of three guide bushings and a ⅛-inch straight inlay bit are needed to get the right relationship of inside, outside, and inlay cuts. The bushing holder that attaches to the router base is also shown.

2. To make the template that will be used to make the circle of makore and the matching hole in the maple, a circle of melamine is cut to the same diameter as the finished makore circle will be. A circle-cutting router jig works well for this. Three rectangles can be cut at once on the table saw, from melamine, ¾-inch MDF, and ¼-inch plywood, each ¾ inch oversize all around.

The melamine circle is centered precisely on the melamine rectangle and screwed through the circle, through the melamine rectangle, and on into a scrap of plywood underneath. The entire sandwich is clamped together on a workbench to prevent shifting. The smallest guide bushing on the router cuts the hole in the rectangular piece of melamine, with the guide bushing kept snug against the circular template for an accurate cut.

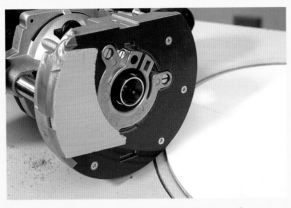

3. A scrap of the template material is taped to the bottom of the router to prevent tipping. Only the rectangular template with the new hole cut out is retained.

4. The rectangular face and backer veneers are cut with a veneer saw by tracing the prepared piece of MDF.

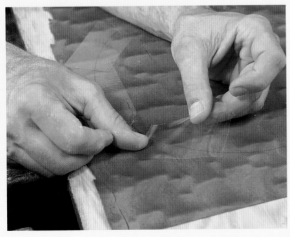

5. Clear packing tape is applied to the makore blank on the router bit's cut path. A scrap of plywood gets clamped underneath to keep the edges of the circle from becoming frayed or broken.

6. To cut the makore circle for the top, the rectangular template is clamped over the blank, and the circle is cut out with the small guide bushing on the router.

7. In a similar way, the template is clamped over the rectangular maple veneer with the edges aligned, and the hole for the makore veneer circle to fit into is cut, this time using the router's largest guide bushing.

8. The makore circle is positioned in the hole of the maple veneer, and they are held together with strips of veneer tape. Then an even coat of Unibond glue is applied to the MDF with a spreader followed by a foam roller.

9. With the face-veneer side of the MDF down, glue is applied to the bottom face and the backer veneer is laid on followed by a release layer of thin plastic, and a ¼-inch platen (with rounded edges that protect the press membrane) goes on each side of the sandwich. Everything is held in alignment with strips of packing tape to minimize shifting when the vacuum is applied.

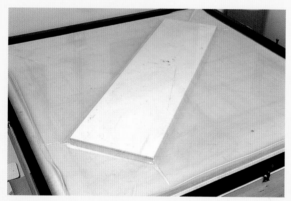

10. As the vacuum is applied, the layers must be checked for alignment. I use a flip-top vacuum table for jobs like this because it's easier to manage than a bag, and it suits the scale of most of my work.

11. After the glue has cured, the veneer tape is removed using warm water and gentle peeling.

12. Glue bleed-through is scraped from the surface, and all the veneer is sanded lightly, checking for a good uniform bond. After cutting all four sides of the veneered piece to finished size on the table saw, biscuit joints are cut to facilitate alignment of the mitered solid wood edging. After the edging has been glued on, the solid wood is carefully scraped just to the level of the veneer. It's best to avoid removing any veneer during this step.

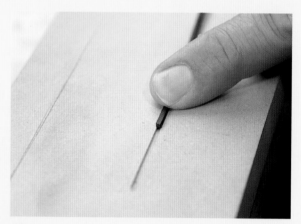

13. Checking the fit of the inlay in a test groove routed in a scrap piece. A dial caliper helps make sure that the router bit and the width of the inlay match. The inlay should be very slightly wider than the groove.

John Clark

14. The width of the inlay is adjusted with a scraper or sandpaper, counting the number of strokes necessary so that the dimension can be repeated. The inlay should protrude slightly above the surface when it is pressed in completely.

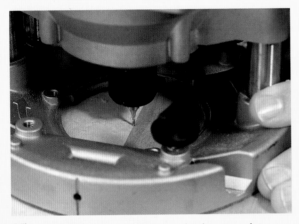

15. With the correct groove and inlay size determined, a clamped straightedge guides the router to cut the inlay grooves in the workpiece, precisely straddling the glue line between the veneered surface and the solid edge. The routing stops at the corners when the grooves nearly intersect.

16. Finishing the square corners, first with a craft knife…

17. …then with a chisel, without changing the dimension of the grooves.

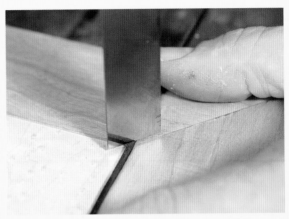

18. One end of the inlay is trimmed with a chisel to fit snugly at the mitered intersection by taking small shavings off the inlay piece until the long point just hits the end of the intersecting groove. The other end of the inlay is then mitered so that the whole piece fits the length of the groove exactly. The inlay isn't pressed in all the way—just enough to check the length.

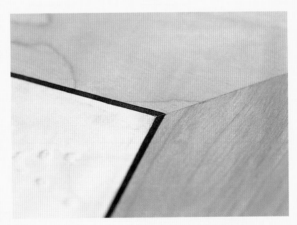

19. Since the short lengths of the inlay are only mitered on one end, they can be left overlong while concentrating on a good fit of the miter with the long piece. When all the straight pieces have been dry fitted, they're pried out of the grooves.

John Clark

20. Yellow glue is spread sparingly on the sides and bottom of one groove at a time.

21. The inlay is pressed in carefully, starting at the mitered ends and working to the center. When multiple pieces of the inlay are needed to complete the run, the ends are mitered progressing as you would in running trim in a house.

22. The inlay is tapped into place with a small hammer and finished by smearing out any bumps with the heel of the hammer. I use a Warrington pattern hammer, because its wide, straight peen is nicely rounded.

23. Strips of masking tape are applied to hold the inlay in place until the glue has dried.

24. For the inlay around the makore circle, the melamine template's circle cutout is positioned over the makore circle on the workpiece. The concentricity is checked by precisely measuring at least three points of the circle. Also, the position of the bit (with the middle-sized guide bushing mounted) should be checked in relation to the veneer joint at several points around the circle to be sure that it will split the glue line.

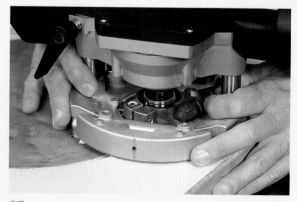

25. The middle-sized guide bushing is used to rout the groove. The same procedure is followed for fitting the inlay as was detailed above for the straight-line inlay.

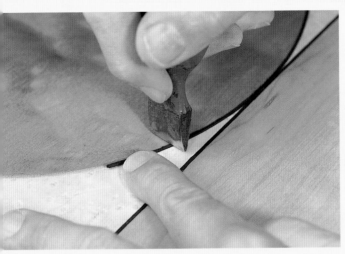

26. The inlay gets pressed in a bit at a time while gently bending it to the curve.

27. When the glue has dried, a cabinet scraper does the initial leveling of the inlay, and a random orbit sander finishes the job.

About the Artist

John Clark's desire to design and make furniture grew out of his frustration as he fretted over every detail of the renovation of an old house he had bought in the late 1970s. When he finally realized that the scale of an entire house was too great to get every element just the way he wanted, he turned to the more manageable dimensions of furniture. Still frustrated by a lack of skills, tools, and too many design ideas, he enrolled in a two-week workshop that dramatically broadened the range of his furniture knowledge, and then he promptly sold the house.

After studying with Wendy Maruyama at the Appalachian Center for Crafts in Smithville, Tennessee, and then at Boston University with Jere Osgood and Alphonse Mattia, Clark opened his own studio in Penland. The excitement of learning every scrap of furniture-making information he could and putting that knowledge to work has been tempered by the reality of raising three kids while paying bills with the pieces he sells. Yet the will to create and discover new techniques has maintained his spirit.

John has exhibited widely in a number of prestigious shows and has placed furniture in several major collections. He has also served as resident artist, wood studio coordinator, and instructor at Penland School of Crafts.

Gallery

The work of these three artists has been both influential and inspirational for me because of their innovative treatment of surfaces and the importance they have each given to surface as a means of detailing and decorating their pieces. Though their methods and materials are diverse and certainly different from my use of veneer, we have all relied on surface decoration in much the same way as centuries of furniture makers before us have done.

Though their graceful forms could allow **Kristina Madsen**'s furniture to stand alone easily in quiet elegance, they also provide a canvas for the rich textures and manipulated surfaces that she uses to give them a much more complex identity. From a distance, the form draws us in, and then the irresistible surface rewards our touch. She began this trend of embellishing surfaces through machine techniques: repetitive cuts from saws or routers, cutting the panels apart, then shifting those components to complicate the surface and give it depth with richness. The additional dust, noise, and tedious mathematical nature of that work, beyond what is required to make the furniture's structure, drove her to pursue a Fulbright grant that allowed her a year of study with a traditional paddle carver in Fuji. The application of that exotic experience transformed the nature of her surface treatment as well as her work style. She now spends much of her work time cross-legged on the floor, cradling the workpiece or kneeling over it for leverage as she carefully wields her chip-carving tools in a Zen-like quiet.

KRISTINA MADSEN
Side Chair, 1989

38 x 20 x 18 inches (96.5 x 50.8 x 45.7 cm)
Pau ferro, silk
PHOTO © MUSEUM OF FINE ARTS, BOSTON, MASSACHUSETTS,
DEPARTMENT OF PHOTOGRAPHIC SERVICES
COLLECTION OF MUSEUM OF FINE ARTS, BOSTON,
MASSACHUSETTS

I was first introduced to the notion of craftsmanship as an art form by **Michael Pierschalla**'s example when we were students together. He quickly became an unofficial teacher and mentor, as his work demonstrated the thoughtful consideration and the significance of details properly executed. When he died in 2002, he left a legacy of work that reflects precise technical prowess and inspired architectural influence. Michael preached that, intentionally or not, every maker's work reflects his/her individual outlook and how he lives his life. His own work was driven by a reverence for craftsmanship, and he believed that quality of construction and details can be a credible basis for determining the success of a piece. His work goes well beyond that, demonstrating a deep understanding of fundamental design principles, color, and form.

Color and texture have been the foundation of **Tom Loeser**'s work, almost from the beginning of his furniture-making career. Though classically trained in a university program, he never conformed to the rituals of complicated joinery or traditional finishes. The genius of his work soars beyond its playfulness and muted color. The careful consideration of layered paint and precise texturing are only the means for his subtle commentary on furniture's fundamental role in our lives. He reminds us that furniture's evolution is cyclic by reinterpreting traditional and archetypal pieces with animated flair.

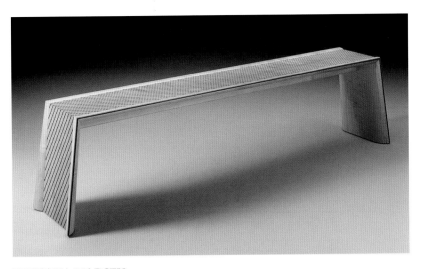

KRISTINA MADSEN

Bench, 1989

16 x 62 x 12 inches (40.6 x 157.5 x 30.5 cm)
Curly maple, ebony
PHOTO © DEAN POWELL

KRISTINA MADSEN

Window Seat, 1990

32 x 50 x 14 inches (81.3 x 127 x 35.6 cm)
Wenge, holly
PHOTO © MICHAEL ZIDE
COLLECTION OF RHODE ISLAND SCHOOL
OF DESIGN MUSEUM, PROVIDENCE, RI

KRISTINA MADSEN

Cabinet on Stand, 1987

53 x 36 x 15 inches (134.6 x 91.4 x 38.1 cm)
Wenge, ebony, obsidian
PHOTO © DAVID RYAN

KRISTINA MADSEN
Painted Chest, detail, 2005

28¾ x 41 x 13½ inches (73 x 104.1 x 34.3 cm)
Maple, milk paint, gesso, pau amarello
PHOTO © DAVID STANSBURY

KRISTINA MADSEN
Chest of Drawers, detail, 2001

54 x 46¼ x 23 inches (137.2 x 117.5 x 58.4 cm)
Bubinga, pau amarello, dyed pearwood veneer, ebony
PHOTO © DAVID STANSBURY

MICHAEL PIERSCHALLA
Tables, circa 1983–1990

PHOTO © ESTATE OF THE ARTIST

John Clark

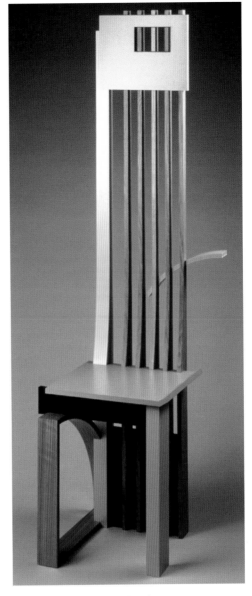

MICHAEL PIERSCHALLA
Chair, circa 1983–1990

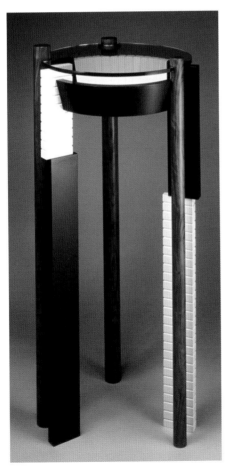

MICHAEL PIERSCHALLA
Table, circa 1983–1990

TOM LOESER

Tripod Chest #2, 1984

62 x 40 x 42 inches (157.5 x 101.6 x 106.7 cm)
Wood, paint, laminate
PHOTO © ARTIST

TOM LOESER

Multiple Complications, 1995

50 x 34 x 21 inches (127 x 86.4 x 53.3 cm)
Zebrawood, paint
PHOTO © ARTIST

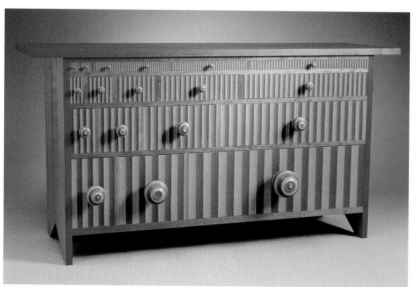

TOM LOESER

Concentration, 1994

32 x 65 x 20 inches (81.3 x 165.1 x 50.8 cm)
Cherry, paint
PHOTOS © ARTIST

John Clark

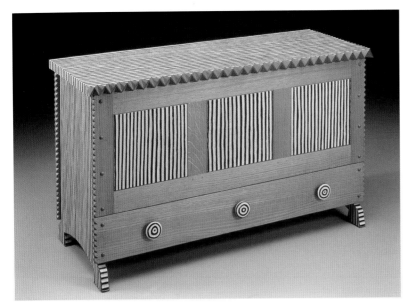

TOM LOESER
Chest over Drawer, 1989

29 x 46 x 18 inches (73.7 x 116.8 x 45.7 cm)
White oak, paint
PHOTO © ARTIST

TOM LOESER
Chair³, 2003

Dimensions variable
Maple, mahogany, paint
PHOTO © ARTIST

John Clark

Kurt Nielsen

By reviving the ancient tradition—carried from the
Egyptians to Chippendale and beyond—of using
realistic animal imagery in furniture, Kurt Nielsen
has carved a niche for himself in contemporary
studio furniture making. His figures are integrated
with his furniture forms, enforcing the impression
that a particular table or chest couldn't exist
without them. Kurt demonstrates how he moves
from rough delineation to final carving of the
pupils of the eyes to enliven his human figures.

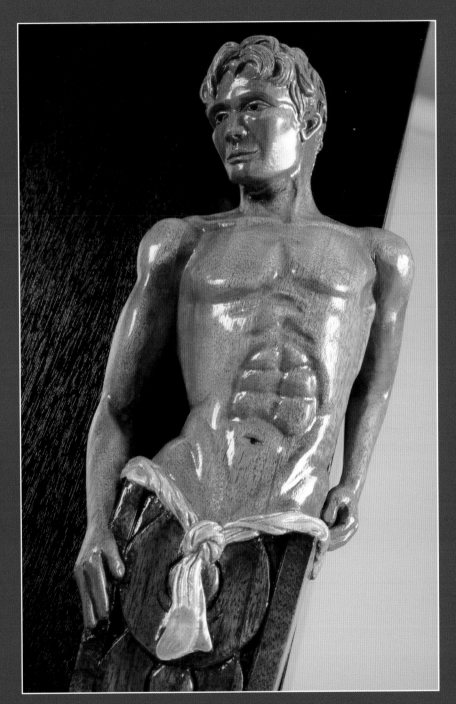

KURT NIELSEN
Introspect, 2005

36 x 20 x 20 inches (91.4 x 50.8 x 50.8 cm)
Mahogany, African sapele, 23-karat gold leaf

Pupils Last

I *love* furniture.
I *love* sculpture.
I *love* it when the two are balanced to form a piece that serves a needed and logical function, is visually engaging, and can take you on a little adventure in your mind if you are willing.

Furniture has so much symbolism and meaning in our homes, our lives, and our culture, yet we often take our domestic objects for granted. For me all these objects are canvases for expression of our selves, our stories, our sensibilities, and our histories. These things convey to others who we are and remind us of where we've been, what we've experienced, and who we've met. Therefore, I aim to create furniture that demands to be seen and has such a presence that it does not allow itself to be ignored in the usual, mundane domestic landscape. I attempt to do so by integrating design, craftsmanship, function, and narrative, and to illustrate the content with vivid figurative sculpture.

Furniture is generally thought of as the thing on which art is displayed, rather than the art itself. I've always resented this notion. However, because of my resistance to making sculpture that sits on a pedestal, I began to integrate my sculptures into the pedestal, so to speak, by thinking of furniture as a canvas on which I could paint with sculpture.

My work is a balance of design, artistic expression, function, and client concerns. Working with clients to design a piece for a specific space has become one of the more challenging and rewarding parts of my process. Nothing exists on a seamless, 80-percent gray, perfectly lit backdrop, like so many of the images and museum pieces we marvel at. Rather, it exists in an interior space, with

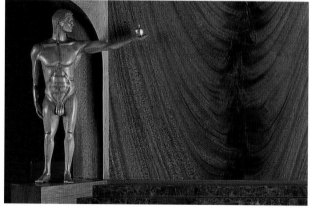

KURT NIELSEN
Adam & Eve Secretary, 2002

62 x 48 x 24 inches (157.5 x 121.9 x 61 cm)
Mahogany, crotch mahogany, amboyna burl, maple, 23-karat gold leaf
PHOTOS © DAVID RAMSEY

KURT NIELSEN
Guardian Dog Credenza, 2000

48 x 60 x 16 inches (121.9 x 152.4 x 40.6 cm)
Maple, madrone burl, linden wood
PHOTOS © DAVID RAMSEY.

walls and colors and drapes and other objects, and with constantly changing natural light. Designing for an existing space is far more challenging than designing a piece in a void.

An additional challenge is creating room for expression and spontaneity within the parameters of the piece itself. I like to think I'm an in-the-moment kind of guy who likes to work from the gut. When I see something that amuses or befuddles me, or that may or may not reflect something from my own life, I twist the truth a little and attempt to weave it into my work. I'm not necessarily concerned about what furniture form the concept manifests, unless the overall meaning influences it. My greatest concern is that the story—or just enough of a story—is conveyed so that a viewer is engaged to stop and ponder for a moment.

The *Guardian Dog Credenza* has that kind of story. I knew a little Chihuahua while I was living in New York, whose owner dressed him in a black leather biker jacket. This was amusing to me. So perfect for a Chihuahua—the little guy with a bad attitude and something to prove. I envisioned that

little dog riding a Harley Davidson motorcycle, and that image led to the motorcycle monkeys in the movie *The Wiz*, which in turn led me to the flying monkeys in the *Wizard of Oz*. Eureka!! Winged Chihuahuas. So I thought to myself, winged Chihuahuas with attitudes? They're going to need sharp, chiseled, stylized, quasi-Deco features to enhance the attitude, which means they will need a Deco-inspired piece to adorn. So I waited for the next client who had Deco tendencies. This particular client was looking for a piece for his home office in which to store files, and a reference library, and it couldn't be more than 4 feet high to fit underneath a painting. There were my parameters. Files, shelving, some secret compartments, and a couple of flying Chihuahuas—yes! That is how I operate. I define the content or story, I let the mood or attitude of the content set the style, and then I balance the style of the piece with the client's needs, interior space, and sense of humor.

Regardless of how much I enjoy exploring furniture, sculpture, and narrative, carving is the foundation of all that I do. Through carving I am able to

KURT NIELSEN
Minotaur Morning Console Cabinet, 2001

32 x 36 x 20 inches (81.3 x 91.4 x 50.8 cm)
African satinwood, mahogany, pommelle sapele,
14-karat gold

KURT NIELSEN
Eduardo & Guiseppi Penguin Bench, 1994

34 x 68 x 28 inches (86.4 x 172.7 x 71.1 cm)
Maple, linden
PHOTOGRAPHER UNKNOWN

tell my stories, and carving is the added dimension of my design vocabulary that distinguishes me from many other furniture makers. The images I see in my head are three-dimensional, and the things that attract my attention in the world are three-dimensional, so simply to draw or paint on furniture would not do. Carving the things I see in my head brings them to life. Once carved, they occupy space and so seem to live.

My first love in the arts was dance. After an embarrassing, painful, entertaining realization in the fourth grade that I was not a dancer myself, I came to love what the human figure could express through movement, posture, and facial expression. The desire to express our human condition through figurative sculpture is at the core of my addiction to making.

Carving the human figure can be an intimidating venture. The greatest obstacle I have found in myself and in my students is critiquing one's own work too harshly. So I remember the words of Paul Sasso, one of the corrupt minds that reached me at an impressionable time in my career: "Make seven

things a week and throw out six." And if that doesn't do it for me, I remember the words of Bob Trotman: "Form doesn't follow function—form follows fuck-up!" In other words, allow yourself to push the boundaries and make mistakes. I was also fortunate to have misspent my youth watching an overabundance of Saturday morning cartoons. This served me well. Because my early explorations into the figure were cartoonish in nature, it was not as evident when I failed to achieve realistic proportions. This also helped me get around the paralyzing obstacle of self-criticism. Four semesters of life drawing and two semesters of anatomy in college also helped enormously in training my eye to discern proportions.

I carve like I draw. If you have had drawing classes, you know of gesture drawing, a five-second scribble that defines the gesture, movement, or flow of a figure. Next, I sketch in the larger anatomy and then detail it with the facial expression, hands, and feet. This is precisely how I carve. When you stand before a block of wood, it can be hard to convince yourself that you know what you are going after.

So I remind myself that wood is a renewable resource, and I give myself permission to screw it all up. Then I attack.

Some days I think I design furniture just as an excuse to carve, and that may be true. I tend to view my design process as a road map that I use to assure myself that everything fits correctly and that the narrative is integrated into the piece and not applied. I view the carving as the journey.

Depending on the size of the piece to be carved, I use either a side grinder with a chainsaw attachment or a pneumatic grinder with a coarse bit to hog off the wood in broad sweeps. I try to work the entire piece at once, avoiding the urge to focus in on one area. I work quickly to force myself to trust my instincts and to save time, energy, and my attention span for detailing, when I will really need them. You can easily burn yourself out during the roughing-out phase. It can be physically exhausting, so I go pell-mell until I can just see the gesture and the separation of the anatomy. I then break out the chisels and try to latch onto any one part of the figure, generally the torso. I try to define its form and gesture just to the point at which I can see it, not to the degree that I am defining the muscles or navel. Then I move to the head, arms, and legs, defining each as they relate to the torso. I am constantly drawing and redrawing on the wood to measure and scale the proportions. Once each element is loosely defined, I scan the piece for unreadable areas. The right arm may be wider than the left, or the transition from the arm to the torso just doesn't look right. I go around and around the piece in this manner, cleaning up and defining here and there in an attempt to work the whole piece at once. I have found that when I carve an arm to near completion and then carve the torso, then the head, then a leg, and so on, the figure looks more like a pieced-together Frankenstein monster than whatever I was going after.

Once I have nailed down the proportions and gesture, and have defined the gross anatomy, then, and only then, will I begin to detail the face, hair, hands, and feet. As a ritual I carve the pupils last, for that moment is when the piece comes to life for me.

KURT NIELSEN
Seven Wonders, a Biomorphic Library, 2002

64 x 23 x 23 inches (162.6 x 58.4 x 58.4 cm)
Mahogany, pommelle sapele, rubber wood, 23-karat gold, clay, silk, mica, assortment of natural objects, books by Daniel Essig
PHOTOS © WALTER MONTGOMERY

KURT NIELSEN
Ages of Man Console Table, 2003

30 x 62 x 20 inches (76.2 x 157.5 x 50.8 cm)
Mahogany, African sapele, 23-karat gold leaf, maple

Hands On

As a rare practitioner of the art of figure carving on furniture, Kurt Nielsen has established a place for himself amidst the variety of contemporary makers with the integrity and energy of his forms. He demonstrates the need to develop the figure as a whole, rather than concentrating on one area at a time. He employs power tools to quickly reveal the figure before refining it by hand.

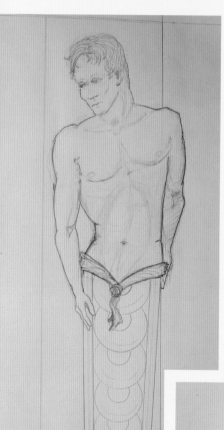

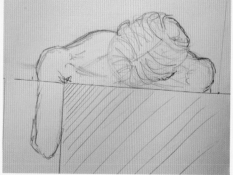

1. I always draw front, side, and top views to help me understand the form and to lay out the joinery.

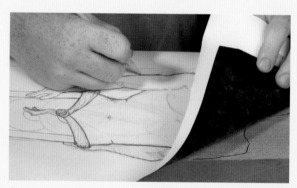

2. The drawing is transferred to the wood using carbon paper.

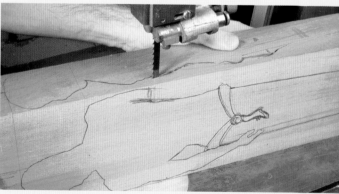

3. I use a band saw to cut the side profile.

4. The cutoff pieces are saved and taped back in place to restore the drawings on the side and to support the workpiece.

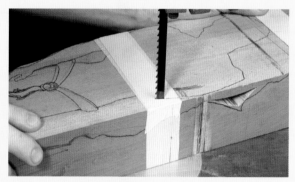

5. The band saw is used to cut the front profile.

6. An arsenal of tools, including a side grinder, a pneumatic die-grinder, planes, and rasps, helps separate the forms of the carving (i.e. the column from the waistband, from the torso, from the neck, and so on).

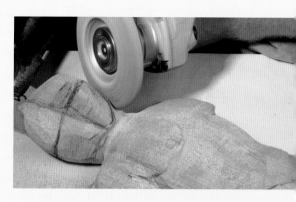

7. The side grinder with a carbide burr bit is used to rough out the larger forms: the torso, arms, and head.

8. The pneumatic die-grinder gets into the tight areas to further rough out the figure.

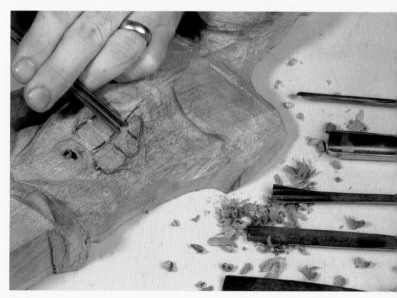

9. Once the roughing out is complete, drawing directly on the figure guides the carving. Choosing appropriately sized gouges for the scale of the piece helps make the carving more precise.

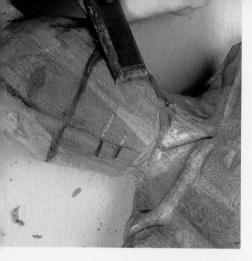

10. I begin by carving the face in the form of a shield, with a ridge running down the center. This center ridge defines where the head is looking and retains material for the nose. A horizontal centerline defines the eye location.

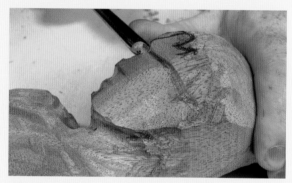

11. After drawing the side profile of the face, the low areas, such as the bridge of the nose, upper lip, and chin, are carved away.

12. The face gets redrawn several times during carving. Constantly shifting one's viewpoint from side to side and from front to top ensures that the face is symmetrical and proportional.

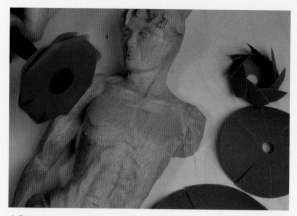

13. A 120- or 150-grit sanding disc is cut into 8 to 12 pie wedges without cutting into the center hole, and the wedges are folded so that they all overlap in the same direction. The sanding disc mounted onto a mandrel in a die-grinder flutter sands the carving. This type of sander follows the contours of the carving and quickly blends out chisel and grinding marks.

14. After flutter sanding, micro V-gouges and veiners add the final detailing of the face, hair and hands.

15. Hand sanding is preferable for the final cleanup.

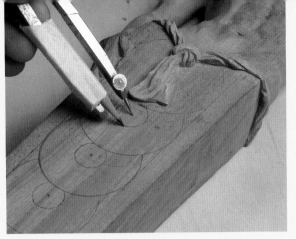

16. A compass is used to lay out the cascading circles that will be carved in the column.

17. The lines are traced with a V-gouge, carving about ⅛-inch deep.

18. A shallow gouge carves a hollow in the outer disc, tapering it down below the disc above it so that the discs appear to lie on top of each other in a cascading fashion.

19. After this area is flutter sanded, a small veiner distinguishes between the center button and the outer disc and accentuates the curve by carving a curved line in the hollow.

20. Now that the figure and column are carved, I mount the column as it will be on the piece in order to lay out the other arm.

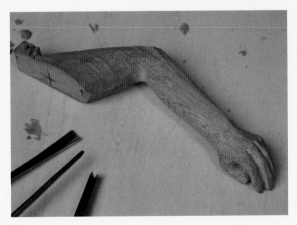

21. The arm is band-sawn and carved as close to finished as possible, leaving some bulk at the joint to carve after it is assembled. I leave a small tab at the top of the arm so the clamp will have something to grab on to.

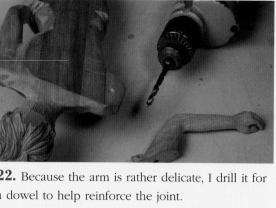

22. Because the arm is rather delicate, I drill it for a dowel to help reinforce the joint.

23. The arm is glued and clamped.

24. The arm is blended into the shoulder and given a final sanding.

25. Only when the figure is complete do I carve in the pupils.

26. To finish the piece, the column section is first stained carefully to avoid spattering onto the figure.

27. I apply three coats of shellac and rub the shellac out with fine steel wool before I apply the size (the "glue" for gold leaf).

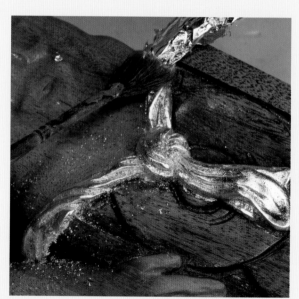

28. After the size has dried, the gold leaf is applied using a soft-bristled brush to push the leaf into the recesses and to ensure proper adhesion.

Kurt Nielsen

29. Two more coats of shellac protect the leaf. Then I like to use tinted lacquers to enhance my carvings. I spray on thin coats of a darker hue and rub them off with superfine steel wool, leaving the tint in the crevices and valleys of the carving.

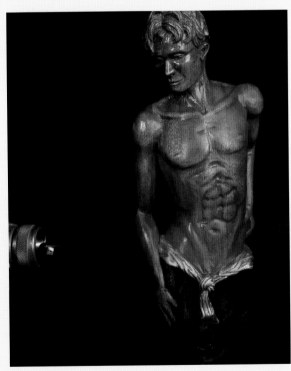

30. Finally, several coats of clear lacquer are sprayed over the entire piece.

About the Artist

Kurt Nielsen maintains his sculpture/furniture studio in Belmont, North Carolina. In addition, he has infiltrated the North Carolina furniture industry over the years, posing as a designer, product development engineer, and production manager, to steal secrets of CNC (computer numerical control) technology for his greater mission of uniting technology and craftsmen to elevate craft from street fairs and local galleries to the global marketplace and world domination via *Art*.

In 2005 Kurt was invited to Japan by the Japanese government to assess the furniture of the Iwayado Tansu craftsmen (government-certified craftsmen working within a 400-year-old tradition) and to evaluate the suitability of their work for the American market.

In 2002 he received the North Carolina Visual Arts Fellowship and in 2001, the Mecklenburg Regional Artist Grant. Kurt has taught workshops at Penland School of Crafts, at Arrowmont, and at Anderson Ranch Art Center.

Kurt's work has been shown extensively in art galleries and museums around the nation, including the Academy of Natural Sciences, Southern Alleghenies Museum of Art, Fuller Museum of Art, Anchorage Museum of History and Art, Leigh Yawkey Woodson Art Museum, and the Elliot Museum.

Kurt has written articles and lectured on emerging technologies that are affecting both craft and the furniture industry. His work has also been published in The Furniture Society's *Tradition in Contemporary Furniture*, Dona Meilach's *Wood Art Today*, and a number of magazines.

Gallery

The entire **McGlauchlin** family—glass artist Tom, ceramicist Pat, and their children, mixed-media artists Chris and Jennifer—got to me at an early age and sufficiently planted the seeds of invention, creation, play, and craftsmanship in my adolescent mind. Their commitment to making and their spirit of making, without reservation or guilt for enjoying themselves and laughing so much, set me on course for a career in the arts before the age of three.

I learned early on in my career that to look at furniture as inspiration for furniture was incestuous and that the offspring of such intercourse was questionable. Still, I haven't always been able to resist. Two furniture makers who made lasting impressions on the way I approach furniture, and whose work broke through the barriers of function to sit proudly as both art and furniture, were **Judy Kensley McKie** and **Bob Trotman**. Judy's ability to explore animal imagery playfully yet control the urge to go functionless was truly the impetus for my own career. She explores relationships and pattern to create a dialogue within a piece, poetically and almost audibly. Bob Trotman was also a pivotal influence; he gave me the courage to incorporate the realistic human figure into my creations, to work BIG, and to feel fairly comfortable throwing function to the wind.

Bookmaker **Dan Essig** has an uncanny ability to find the tiniest of living things in ordinary places and to know what they are called. This ability to see little creatures smaller than a toenail clipping hidden in the grass while standing 6 feet 4 inches tall inspires me and reminds me that there is a whole other world worth exploring just outside the confines of my own head.

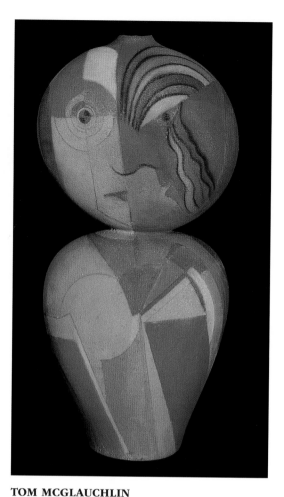

TOM MCGLAUCHLIN
Conversation with Tears, 2005

Height, 17 inches (43.2 cm)
Glass, underfired enamels, pastels, colored pencils
PHOTO © ARTIST

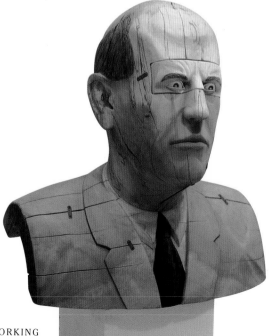

BOB TROTMAN
Tom, 2005

29 x 26 x 20 inches (73.7 x 66 x 50.8 cm)
Poplar, basswood, steel, tempera
PHOTO © ARTIST

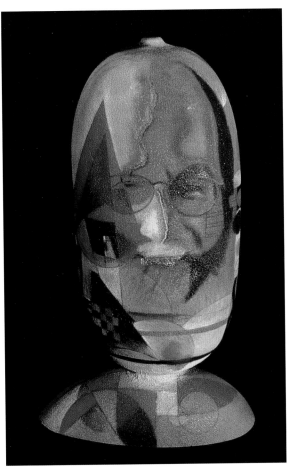

TOM MCGLAUCHLIN
Kandinsky and Me, 1995

20 x 13 x 5 inches (50.8 x 33 x 12.7 cm)
Glass, underfired enamels, pastels, colored
pencils; design transferred from digital print
PHOTO © ARTIST

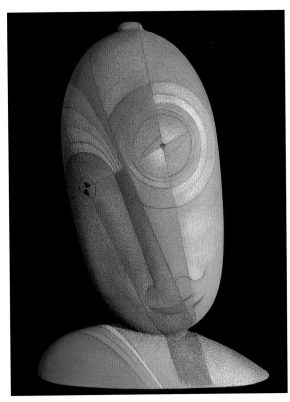

TOM MCGLAUCHLIN
The Skeptic, 1998

19 x 11 x 5 inches (48.3 x 27.9 x 12.7 cm)
Glass, underfired enamels, pastels, colored pencils
PHOTO © ARTIST

TOM MCGLAUCHLIN
Woman on Wabash Street, 2005

15 x 13 x 5 inches (38.1 x 33 x 12.7 cm)
Glass, underfired enamels, pastels, colored pencils
PHOTO © ARTIST

CHRIS MCGLAUCHLIN
Hand and Eye Coordination, 1982

17 x 12 inches (43.2 x 30.5 cm)
Colored pencil, paper
PHOTO © ARTIST

CHRIS MCGLAUCHLIN
The Artist's Studio, 1982

17 x 12 inches (43.2 x 30.5 cm)
Colored pencil, paper
PHOTO © ARTIST

JENNIFER MCGLAUCHLIN
Self Portrait, 1987

19 x 14 inches (48.3 x 35.6 cm)
India ink, paper
PHOTO © ARTIST

JUDY KENSLEY MCKIE
Jaguar Bench, 1992

27 x 61 x 16 inches (68.6 x 154.9 x 40.6 cm)
Bronze; cast
PHOTO © EVA HEYD

JUDY KENSLEY MCKIE
Rabbit Sideboard, 2004

32 x 64 x 18 inches
(81.3 x 162.6 x 45.7 cm)
Bronze, glass; cast
PHOTO © SCOTT MCCUE

JUDY KENSLEY MCKIE
Monkey Chair, 1994

36 x 25 x 25 inches (91.4 x 63.5 x 63.5 cm)
Bronze, walnut; cast, carved
PHOTO © SCOTT MCCUE

Kurt Nielsen

DANIEL ESSIG
Bits Sacred Geometry, 2003

15 x 12 x 2 inches (38.1 x 30.5 x 5.1 cm)
Mahogany, paint, drill bits, mica, fossil; carved
PHOTO © ARTIST

DANIEL ESSIG
Relic Sacred Geometry, detail, 2004

10 x 12 x 2 inches (25.4 x 30.5 x 5.1 cm)
Mahogany, nails, mica, found objects; carved
PHOTO © ARTIST

DANIEL ESSIG
Chained Book, 2004

6 x 4 x 3 inches (15.2 x 10.2 x 7.6 cm)
Mahogany, milk paint, handmade paper, mica,
linen thread, brass, shells
PHOTO © ARTIST

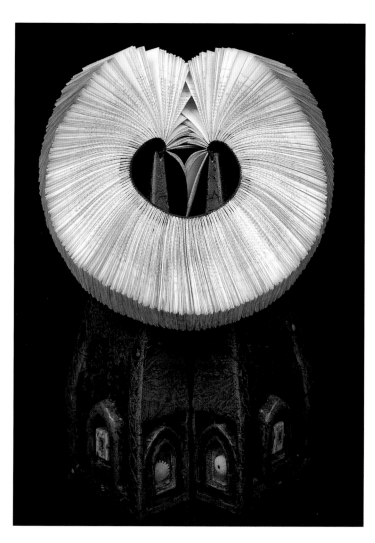

DANIEL ESSIG
Amulet Bridge Book, 2005

23 x 19 x 9½ inches (58.4 x 48.3 x 24.1 cm)
Mahogany, paint, spalted maple, 19th-century rag text
paper, tin, mica, shells; carved
PHOTOS © ROBIN DREYER

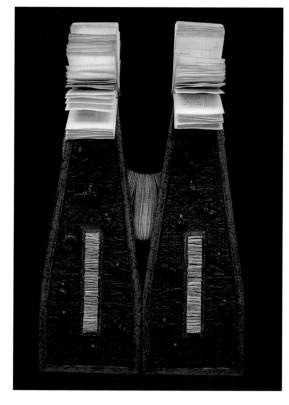

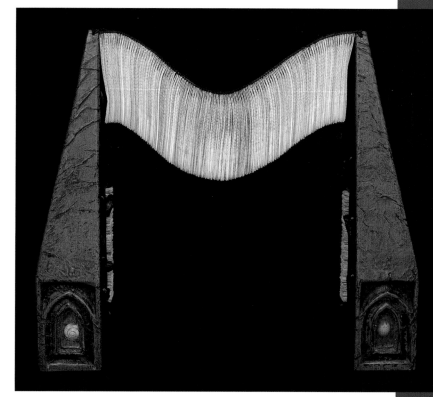

Kurt Nielsen

Since childhood I have been awed, horrified, and inspired by the nameless, centuries-old craftsmen and masons who so impishly carved life into the otherwise mundane architectural details of cities around the world.

— Kurt Nielsen

PHOTOS © KURT NIELSEN

Kurt Nielsen

Penland School of Crafts Overview

enland School of crafts is a national center for craft education located in the mountains of North Carolina. Penland's mission is to support individual and artistic growth through craft. Penland offers one-, two-, and eight-week adult workshops in books and paper, clay, drawing and painting, glass, iron, metals, photography, printmaking, textiles, and wood. The school also sponsors artists' residencies, a community education program, and a craft gallery representing artists affiliated with the school.

Penland School was founded by Lucy Morgan, a teacher at an Episcopalian school that once occupied several buildings which are still part of Penland. In 1923, she organized the Penland Weavers, to provide looms, materials, and instruction to local women and market their handwoven goods. She invited noted weaving expert Edward F. Worst to teach, and when requests for instruction came from other parts of the country, Penland

School was born. Soon after the first students arrived in 1929, other crafts were added, and the school began to raise funds, acquire property, and construct buildings.

When Lucy Morgan retired in 1962, she was succeeded by Bill Brown. During Brown's 21-year tenure, new media, such as iron and glass, were added to the program and the school began offering eight-week sessions in the spring and fall. Brown also started the resident artist program, which provides low-cost housing and studios to craft artists who work at Penland for several years, and he began a work-study scholarship program to make Penland accessible to a broader range of students.

Today the school encompasses 43 buildings located on 400 acres of land. Each year approximately 1,200 people come to Penland for instruction and another 12,000 pass through as visitors. Penland has no standing faculty; its instructors include full-time studio artists as well as teachers from colleges and universities. Students live at Penland and take only one class at a time, allowing them to learn by total immersion—the ideas and information gained in a two-week session might take a year to absorb and process.

The school has also become the focal point for a lively community of craft artists, thanks in part to the resident program which has encouraged many artists to settle in the area. The presence of so many nearby studios greatly enhances the quality of the student experience.

Students come from all walks of life. They range from 19 to 90 years of age and from absolute beginners to professional craftspeople. Some see Penland as a productive retreat, some as a source of inspiration for their personal creative lives, and others as a place to exchange vital information about material, technique, and process. What brings them all together is a love of materials and making, and the often transformative experience of working with intensity and focus in a supportive community atmosphere.

Penland School began out of a strong belief in a few simple values. Lucy Morgan summarized these as "the joy of creative occupation and a certain togetherness—working with one another in creating the good and the beautiful." For more than 75 years, these principles have guided a remarkable institution which has had a pervasive influence on American craft and touched the lives of thousands of individuals.

For more information about Penland School of Crafts, call 828-765-2359 or visit www.penland.org.

Acknowledgments

Lark Books is proud to present *The Penland Book of Woodworking* as the fourth in a series of joint efforts with Penland School of Crafts. The completion of such an intricate project is truly a collaboration. It is through the extraordinary contributions made by the wonderful people connected to Penland that we have been able to bring this book to fruition.

Recognition, first, must go to the artists Curtis Buchanan, John Clark, Jenna Goldberg, Kurt Nielsen, Craig Nutt, Jere Osgood, Michael Puryear, Paul M. Sasso, Doug Sigler, and Brent Skidmore. Their willingness to commit to this project is inspiring. Not only did they endure the pressure of meeting publishing deadlines to deliver both written and visual material, they did so while teaching workshops, lecturing, exhibiting, and continuing to produce their own creative work. It is in light of their effort, dedication, talent, and can-do attitudes that we say they were all a joy to work with.

We are grateful to the artists and institutions that contributed gallery images. Their intriguing work significantly enhances the contents of each chapter.

Jean W. McLaughlin, director of Penland School of Crafts, enthusiastically endorsed the book, and other key Penland staff members were instrumental in bringing the book to publication. Our thanks go to Dana Moore, Penland program director, who acted as the school's liaison through the many months of production, and who made the initial contacts with the artists. Robin Dreyer, communications manager, and Jeff McLarty, wood studio coordinator, along with Dana Moore, provided much helpful insight with the manuscript review. John Clark took time to act as technical manuscript consultant, for which we are grateful.

Lark Books art director Kristi Pfeffer shaped the book's distinctive visual style with contributions from talented photographers from across the United States. Special thanks also to Shannon Yokeley, associate art director, for her steadfast help.

Thomas Stender, *Editor*
Nathalie Mornu, *Associate Editor*

For more information about Penland School of Crafts, call (828) 765-2359 or visit www.penland.org.

Contributing Photographers

Jonathan Binzen photographed Michael Puryear in his furniture studio located in Shokan, New York.

Andrew Bredar documented Paul Sasso's painting process, and photographed his finished work.

Jeff Cravotta set up photography in Kurt Nielsen's Belmont, North Carolina, studio; Kurt's wife, **Tricia Nielsen,** composed the shots and snapped the shutter during the month-long process of carving *Introspect*.

Mark Johnston photographed Jenna Goldberg at work in her Providence, Rhode Island, studio. He also took pictures of the finished pieces featured in this book.

Darlene Kaczmarczyk shot the images of Brent Skidmore and some of his finished work. The shoot took place in Brent's studio, located in Grand Rapids, Michigan.

Steve Mann photographed the process shots for both John Clark and Doug Sigler in their respective studios in Penland, North Carolina. Steve also took pictures of some of Doug's finished work and site-specific pieces.

Tom Raymond served as the photographer for Curtis Buchanan's chapter.

Andrew Virzi photographed the pictures of Jere Osgood's technique section.

Deborah Wiygul documented Craig Nutt's process in his Kingston Springs, Tennessee, studio.

Contributing Artists

Elizabeth Alexander
Charlotte, North Carolina
Pages 49, 50

John D. Alexander Jr.
Baltimore, Maryland
Page 87

Barbara Bayne
Montague, Massachusetts
Page 128

Bill Brown Sr.
Linville Falls, North Carolina
Page 105

Ted Blachly
Warner, New Hampshire
Page 157

Brian Boggs
Berea, Kentucky
Page 89

Marcel Breuer
Deceased
Page 109

Wendell Castle
Scottsville, New York
Pages 105, 106

Mark Del Guidice
Norwood, Massachusetts
Page 70

Robert Diemert
Dundas, Ontario, Canada
Page 70

John Dodd
Canandaigua, New York
Pages 68, 107, 108

David N. Ebner
Bellport, New York
Page 152

Daniel Essig
Asheville, North Carolina
Pages 214, 215

Amy Forsyth
New Hope, Pennsylvania
Page 31

Tage Frid
Deceased
Page 105

Lanie Gannon
Nashville, Tennessee
Page 51

Blaise Gaston
Earlysville, Virginia
Page 151

Stephan Goetschius
Layton, New Jersey
Pages 48, 49

Bobby Hansson
Rising Sun, Maryland
Page 175

Rob Hare
Ulster Park, New York
Page 71

Stephen Hogbin
Wiarton, Ontario, Canada
Page 27

Barbara Holmes
Oakland, California
Page 130

Michelle Holzapfel
Marlboro, Vermont
Page 29

Michael Hosaluk
Saskatoon, Saskatchewan, Canada
Pages 53, 131

Thomas Hucker
Jersey City, New Jersey
Page 150

Evan Hughes
Brooklyn, New York
Page 69

Michael Hurwitz
Philadelphia, Pennsylvania
Page 152

Daniel Jackson
Deceased
Page 149

Arthur Jones
Winter Park, Florida
Page 28

Richard Judd
Paoli, Wisconsin
Page 68

Kim Kelzer
Freeland, Washington
Pages 30, 31

William A. Keyser Jr.
Victor, New York
Pages 110, 111

Drew Langsner
Marshall, North Carolina
Page 87

R. T. Leverich
Olympia, Washington
Page 111

Tom Loeser
Madison, Wisconsin
Pages 194, 195

Thomas Lynch
Rock Cave, West Virginia
Page 88

Kristina Madsen
Southhampton, Massachusetts
Pages 171, 172, 173, 190, 191, 192

Wendy Maruyama
San Diego, California
Page 173

Alphonse Mattia
Westport, Massachusetts
Page 173

Chris McGlauchlin
Toledo, Ohio
Page 213

Jennifer McGlauchlin
Toledo, Ohio
Page 213

Tom McGlauchlin
Toledo, Ohio
Pages 210, 211

Judy Kensley McKie
Cambridge, Massachusetts
Pages 174, 213

John McNaughton
Evansville, Indiana
Pages 26, 27

Carlo Mollino
Deceased
Page 126

Clifton Monteith
Lake Ann, Michigan
Page 127

Andrew Muggleton
Longmont, Colorado
Page 67

Brad Reed Nelson
Aspen, Colorado
Page 133

Will Neptune
Acton, Massachusetts
Page 132

Beeken Parsons
Shelburne, Vermont
Page 156

Timothy S. Philbrick
Narragansett, Rhode Island
Page 155